EDUMAGIC SHINE ON

A Guide for New Teachers

SAMANTHA FECICH   KATY GIBSON

HANNAH SANSOM   HANNAH TURK

EduMatch Publishing

Published by EduMatch®
PO Box 150324, Alexandria, VA 22315
www.edumatchpublishing.com

These books are available at special discounts when purchased in quantities of 10 or more for use as premiums, promotions fundraising, and educational use. For inquiries and details, contact the publisher: sarah@edumatch.org.

ISBN: 978-1-970133-44-8

Contents

Introduction

Picture yourself at your favorite coffee shop. We just ordered our drinks, although they'll probably be cold before we can focus long enough to drink them. You join the four of us at a table. We are all laughing, smiling, and sharing fun stories, like that one time we all traveled to Pittsburgh to attend our first EdCamp. Although we should probably introduce ourselves first; Hannah Sansom, Katy Gibson, Hannah Turk, and Dr. Sam Fecich.

Hannah S. moved back to her small town in Pennsylvania after college to teach third-grade math . . . in her old third-grade classroom . . . with her very own third-grade teacher. As the sole teacher for this tested subject and completely new to the field, Hannah felt over-whelmed and pressured to do well. She did not spend four years of college preparing for 100+ kiddos. It was a quick mindset adjustment, but Hannah cannot imagine starting her career any other way. She now has her Master of Education degree in reading and math, all because of becoming a math teacher. Hannah is currently beginning her fourth year working alongside her third-grade teacher, who has become a great mentor and friend.

Katy G., for her first year, was a seventh-grade math and life science teacher. However, she moved away from the big city and is now living in a small town. Katy currently teaches sixth-grade science and social studies in a small community. In between her first year and current job, she was a paraprofessional and a fifth-grade long-term substitute all in the same year. Katy is similar to a utility player on a baseball field: she has a big personality, loves comedy, and always looks forward to reminding her students not to blurt out random thoughts during class time.

Hannah T. started her first year as a newlywed, living in her in-law's basement in Virginia. She was bright-eyed and eager to begin teaching first grade when a significant health issue put her in the hospital for the second week of school. Definitely one way to start the school year with a bang! As she worked to get her sea legs in her first year, she also found out she was pregnant . . . well, that complicates things! Through a grueling pregnancy, classroom challenges, and personal life difficulties, she made it through her first year with lots of professional and life lessons learned. She can't wait to share with you her struggles and triumphs.

As a professor in the education department, Dr. Sam Fecich prepares preservice teachers each day to be educators of excellence. She knows as she sends them off into the world, she can't prepare them for everything they are going to face in and out of their classrooms. She lets them go knowing that she did the best she could to prepare them for their future. They have the foundation to flourish and grow and to be great leaders in their classrooms, schools, districts, and around the world. It is so exciting to hear about their plans for post-graduation and their future classrooms. But she knows that the first year of teaching is hard.

This book is designed to help you, as a beginning teacher, thrive during your first year of teaching by asking you to reflect, challenge yourself, and celebrate wins in and out of the classroom. It is hard—yes. But you can do it. You've got this—after all, you are an edumagician. We are starting with expectations. Stop here and think about the expectations that you have for yourself as a teacher, a leader, a learner.

Expectations for myself as a teacher, an educator of excellence:

Expectations for myself as a leader in the classroom, school, and district:

Expectations for myself as a lifelong learner:

Think about what you wrote. The expectations that you have for yourself as a teacher, a leader, and a learner are most likely grand! Be warned, though, these expectations may not always hold true. Life is full of ups and downs, even in the teaching realm. Hannah T. begins by sharing,

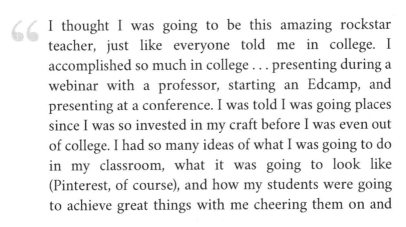

> I thought I was going to be this amazing rockstar teacher, just like everyone told me in college. I accomplished so much in college . . . presenting during a webinar with a professor, starting an Edcamp, and presenting at a conference. I was told I was going places since I was so invested in my craft before I was even out of college. I had so many ideas of what I was going to do in my classroom, what it was going to look like (Pinterest, of course), and how my students were going to achieve great things with me cheering them on and

discovering all of their gifts and strengths. But then my
year began."

The first years of teaching are hard, but years that are worthwhile,
fulfilling, and full of growth! Keep in mind that every veteran teacher
you know has been through their first year. You will, too! You may
find out that you had great expectations but that they never were
fulfilled. Friends, that is why we are here! We have lived it; we have
learned through the trials and joys of being a newbie. We are here to
offer a guide for the first years! Keep this book handy as you will find
yourself coming back to sections, being reflective, and journaling
about the first years. Sit back, grab your coffee, favorite colored pen,
highlighter, some sticky notes/flags, and start this reflective journey.

E: Expectations

EXPECTATIONS. Let's chat about great expectations of teaching — that is a very broad term in the education world. Hannah S. shares,

 Leaving the college life of a pre-service teacher at an academically rigorous college, I expected to walk into a classroom with my head held high because of the experiences college allowed me to have. By the time I graduated, I had ample hours of getting my feet wet in the classroom, over 150 hours! I had a strong resume, already co-organized/created EdCamp Grove City, and presented at conferences. I felt confident as a teacher and as a leader."

Many of you probably feel similarly to Hannah S. You have so many hours of teaching experience. You planned all the lessons, you connected objectives to state standards and back again, and integrated technology in meaningful ways. No matter which university or college you attended, you spent countless hours in methods courses and reading the latest research on the components of teaching (technology, co-teaching, curriculum, etc.). You are feeling ready to teach, to have your own classroom. That is a great feeling to have, friends—don't lose it! As you will learn, there are many components to the art of teaching. We don't just plan lessons and deliver amazing content—we are nurses, counselors, behavior managers, parents . . . the list goes on. Let's begin with how college shaped your expectations as a teacher, leader, and learner.

How did college shape your expectations?

You may have the hours under your belt, but being a teacher is so much more- we want to help you grasp that concept now. Let's explore those components of teaching. Take a moment and list your expectations based on your knowledge and experience as a preservice teacher. Go ahead, we left you some space.

My expectations of teaching based on my preservice teaching experience:

- Just "Know" how to teach the subjects
- Perfect Behavior Management
  ↳ & never have to change
- Make friends
- Know everything about the Law of Special Ed

Alright, so you probably are expecting to have a behavior management technique, or maybe you listed resources and tools needed to incorporate the latest technology. Perhaps you listed supportive colleagues in a professional workplace or access to the resources and tools needed to incorporate the latest technology. Or maybe you dreamt of a collaborative co-teaching experience along with the support of administration and a true mentor teacher. Friends, most of these expectations have been shaped by your experiences in college as a preservice teacher. These aren't wrong, but let's dive into the six common areas together.

The courses designed early in your college career were created to teach you the ins and outs of content delivery, classroom management, differentiated instruction, and educational technology, among other core topics when it comes to teaching. These classes provide you with a solid foundation to build from. Hannah S. shares that ". . . undergrad gave me the tools I needed to blossom into the teacher I am today and will mature into for years to come." We couldn't agree more- your program prepares you with the building blocks of teaching. College or university provides you with the tools to teach, but experience teaches you how and when to use them.

Teacher Expectation 1: Classroom Management

Probably the most challenging component of teaching for first-year teachers is classroom management. There are so many techniques to choose from, and having a classroom of respect and rapport is so important, you want a place where students feel loved, respected, and valued. Even after classes on behavior management and implementing several techniques, Hannah S. shares that as a 22-year-old newbie, she struggled with managing certain behaviors. She explained that what worked with some students did not work with others. That's a given! But how to get through to the students is something that you will always improve upon as each new student walks through your door.

very true!

A cooperating teacher once told her that learning behavior management never ends. Think about that, friends; it is so true! It is one of those things (like parenting) that will come with time and experience. So, what to do when you cannot seem to figure out how to handle certain students or situations? ASK! Find yourself a *true* mentor teacher and see what s/he does in their room. We have all used various techniques: from token economy, to passing out one Skittle (yes, one), to a classroom bank. Figure out what *motivates* your learners and what works with your personality and those of your students. In order to do this, you MUST get to know your students-beyond the student interest survey. It also may be overwhelming to choose the right tool. It may be a trial and error journey. It may not. It just depends. Here a few to get your creative classroom management juices flowing:

- Remember those long hours spent as a kid playing Monopoly? Channel your inner banker and incorporate a token economy or class bank for your students to make deposits and withdraws.
- Think about setting up challenges for your class as a whole, or individual challenges. Provide students with rewards throughout the day, such as providing them with points, a *Go Noodle* (GoNoodle, 2019) break -who doesn't love some McPufferson in the morning?
- Do you have a techy side? Try using technology tools that can help support desired and appropriate behaviors such as Class Dojo, Bloomz, TeacherKit, or Class Craft, to name a few.

Make Magic Happen:

Make a list of behavior management techniques that you have learned. Why have they worked? What methods haven't? Why? Use this section as a reflection area. Add to it as you journey through your first year of teaching. Practice those reflective skills!

Classroom Management Technique:	Did It Work? Why?	Did It NOT Work? Why?
class rewards	yes: frequent tokens (yr 1)	no: larger goals (Yr 2)
Stickers	yes: positive rein.	no: taking away
buoy bucks	yes: positive	no: treasure chest
hole punches	yes: positive & didn't take away	

Teacher Expectation 2: Co-Teaching

Ok, so now we have reflected on our expectations in the realm of classroom management. What happens if you have an #eduawesome classroom management technique implemented with your learners, but it is not followed by your co-teacher? Or what if your co-teacher is more of a back-seat driver, not a co-pilot? How about the reverse? How will you handle conflict as a new teacher vs. a (probably) more experienced, seasoned teacher? You have already learned about the importance of co-teaching in college courses, but it is another component of teaching that is hard to honestly figure out until you are experiencing it yourself.

What are your expectations for an #eduawesome and #edumagical, collaborative co-teaching experience? What are some action steps that you can take to create and cultivate that co-teaching experience? After all, you are working towards the same goal: helping that group of students succeed.

What are your expectations for an #edumagical, collaborative co-teaching experience?

para

- Be on the same page
- Take initiative
- Provide assistance & advice
- Allow me to lead

Unfortunately, co-teaching does not always look the same. Some people have amazing co-teaching experiences- others not so much. Abby M. shares her experience with co-teaching during her first year:

> When you study special education in college, you learn all about co-teaching. You learn about the research that supports it, the benefits of it to all students, and the different models of it. Unfortunately, many school districts are very behind on implementing effective co-teaching. When I stepped into my first year of teaching, I hoped to utilize effective co-teaching models but quickly realized it was not the norm for my district. First, I was handed IEPs with 60 minutes of daily pull-out instruction in the areas of math and reading. Then, when I challenged these minutes, I was told that their standardized test scores were not high enough for inclusion or that they couldn't handle the classroom for behavioral reasons. Finally, when I did start amending IEPs to increase inclusion minutes, I quickly realized that my role would be simply that of a paraprofessional

rather than that of an educator. I sat next to "my" students, assisted them on individual problems they struggled with, and tried to quiet behaviors. It was a bit shocking after spending four years hearing how great inclusion and co-teaching is [sic] for children with disabilities, to see that districts are not adequately training and requiring this best practice."

We would like you to consider our definition of what co-teaching can be. **A true co-teaching experience is one certified general education and one certified special education teacher working together to teach and reach all students. It's not about "his" kids and "her" kids, but it's about *our* class—*our* kids.** Let's focus on those keywords. "Working together to teach and reach all students." How does that look in a dysfunctional co-teaching experience versus a functional one?

There is not a cookie-cutter way of figuring out the best co-teaching experience, but use what you learned in college courses to piece together a collaborative, co-piloting team. We say 'co-piloting team' because both of you are navigating the learning experience to cultivate an environment designed for all students. A successful co-teaching experience is one where the teachers genuinely know and understand the zone of proximal development, ZPD (Woolfolk, 2013), and the schema of the students.

Remember Charlotte Danielson (2007)? As teachers, we are to plan, prepare, and create a classroom of respect and rapport, and we are also expected to be professional and to implement meaningful instruction. Set aside time to actually plan with your co-teacher. You both should be on the same page with the learning goals, current content, scope of where the content is going, and expectations for assessments. Frodo and Sam would never have made it to Middle Earth if they didn't work together, and while you may not be slaying Orcs and hiding from Sauron, you are on your own adventure that needs careful planning for a successful outcome (Tolkien, 1954).

You may find yourself on a bumpy road, not because of needing to modify the content, but because working with your co-teacher may be more difficult than you expected. If a conflict arises between the two of you for any reason, pause and think. Don't make hasty decisions or comments. Don't go complaining to other teachers. Most importantly, don't let things go. If you don't take time and effort to mend conflict, it will only make things harder for you as you go forward in your school year. Remember to be professional even though it may feel awkward to confront a veteran teacher or discuss differences/problems. Consider that if you feel there is a problem, your co-teacher probably recognizes something as well. Friends, keep the lines of communication open between you and your co-teacher. Share the good and the not so good.

If co-teaching does not reflect an experience where both teachers work together to teach and reach all learners, **advocate** for the students! If you are in a co-teaching experience, then you have learners who need additional support. Your students probably won't voice that they aren't getting "co-taught" because if it isn't being done, it probably hasn't been implemented properly in the past. Find someone, a mentor teacher or principal, for example, who can help you advocate for better implementation of co-teaching.

Lastly, take time to build a relationship with your co-teacher. We're not saying that you have to get dinner or go shopping, although you most definitely can! You get to know your students, so why not get to know the person you are teaching with? No, you may not have much in common outside of school, but figure out what makes him or her tick. Hannah S. sat in a professional development where presenters discussed co-teaching and figuring out the "love language" of the other teacher. While you aren't going to be affectionate to your co-teacher in the same way as a spouse would be, ask yourself, does your co-teacher appreciate words of affirmation? Notes? Maybe your co-teacher decompresses with alone time or needs to talk things through after a difficult day. Getting to know your co-teacher on a personal level is a great foundation for cultivating a collaborative co-teaching experience. It will take time to figure out your niche in the realm of co-teaching. Plan together. Work together. Learn together. You never know what you have to learn from another teacher . . . maybe he or she is the next great leader in education, and YOU had the opportunity to learn from them first!

Teacher Expectation 3: Incorporating Technology

We've discussed expectations resulting from college courses on implementing behavior management techniques and cultivating co-teaching experiences. What about all that #edtech stuff? Some of us, meaning authors of this guide, had a very different perspective of technology when it was first introduced in college. There is so much out there, and things are always improving and changing. It can be overwhelming!

We all take a class about educational technology. In fact, that is the course that Dr. Sam teaches preservice teachers K-12 in all subject areas. She shares,

> It is a blast! I truly look forward to it each semester because every time that I teach it—it is NEVER the same class twice! Although most students take the class during their freshman or sophomore year, I work to provide them with resources that they can take with them beyond this one class. I provide them with resources that will carry them through their college careers into their first year of teaching and beyond. I do this by providing them with skills that are transferable from tool to tool. Friends, tools and tech are going to change, but the skills to access them will stay the same."

Tech tools are constantly being added to our toolbox and it can feel overwhelming to stay on top of them all, but as long as we keep our growth mindset and desire to learn, we should have the skills to see ways to apply tech tools in our classroom no matter how cutting edge they may be.

Make Magic Happen:

Follow education movers and shakers who are going to inform your teaching and learning. Follow people who are going to impact your teaching and your career. Don't just follow for the sake of getting a follow-back, but follow people who are going to help you grow, learn, and lead. Being a connected educator is more than just being plugged into social media; share what you are learning with others and gather resources to add to your teacher tool bag. Education is about the give-and-take collaboration with people everywhere! Some of our go-to edtech resources that are tried and true are below. Check out our recommendations, but also add yours to the list too!

Subject Area	Our Recommendations	Your Resources
All grades	❏ https://www.commonsense.org/education/ ❏ https://www.edutopia.org/ ❏ www.chalk.com	
PreK-2	❏ www.spellingcity.com ❏ www.abcya.com ❏ www.kodable.com	*Starfall.com* *nearpod.com*
3-6	❏ www.nearpod.com ❏ www.peardeck.com ❏ www.wizer.me	*Happy Numbers*
8-12	❏ www.classflow.com ❏ www.icivics.com ❏ www.gimkit.com	
Special education	❏ https://www.microsoft.com/en-us/education/products/learning-tools ❏ https://boardmakeronline.com	*Boom learning*

More Resources Here

Alright, some of you may be thinking, *"Wow, these are awesome resources if we have access to the resources and tools, but what happens if you are in a district that does not have the funding to support educational technology?"* That is a great question, my friend. We would recommend speaking to your administration and asking if it's ok to write a grant or two, or three. When writing a grant, focus on the why behind the technology tool. Some questions to think about include:

- What can my students do as a result of using this tech tool?
- What will my students be able to create by using this tool? How will it be shared?
- How can this tool help support ALL learners in the classroom?

Many educators are writing grants or crowdfunding in order to get some tech and other resources for their classrooms. Hannah T. was lucky enough to have a family member in the instructional technology field. He was able to share a few older generation iPads from the foundation he worked for. Think outside the box! Our go-to funding resources are:

PledgeCents	DonorsChoose

Katy G. shares how she used DonorsChoose to accomplish a funding goal. As her first year of teaching started, there were so many supplies that she needed for her students' success. However, as most educators know, many schools cannot provide all the supplies needed for the classrooms, unfortunately. Katy's class sizes averaged 30 students! That's a lot of needs, which means a lot of money. Therefore, she looked to DonorsChoose for some help.

Overall, it is a very easy program to use and worth the time. The most difficult part as a first-year teacher was that she did not have many photos of her classroom. Instead, she used projects that she had students complete in the past. She simply titled the project "Blissful Beginnings," and posted it on all of her social media platforms. She received her funding relatively quickly. Once she received her supplies, she wrote thank-you notes and provided pictures to showcase how the funds had been put to good use.

Shortly after she completed this project, she needed some materials for her level one English to Speakers of Other Languages (ESOL) students in the classroom. She wanted to provide them with Spanish-English picture dictionaries. Yet again, she looked to DonorsChoose.

As a first-year teacher, it is beneficial to take the time to utilize these types of websites. However, be sure to ask administrators first, since there may be school policies regarding fundraising.

Another resource to try to help fund your classroom is a crowdfunding movement that started in the summer of 2019 called #Clear-TheLists. A teacher in Texas named Courtney Jones began the movement to help out her own classroom for the new school year. It was a simple concept: Create an Amazon wishlist, share it with the Facebook Group 'Support A Teacher—#clearthelists,' and then gift at least one other teacher. However, as the movement grew, teachers were encouraged to take their lists to Twitter in hopes of getting their wishlist cleared. Celebrities even helped the movement's visibility! Khloe Kardashian encouraged others to help donate to teachers' classrooms and used the hashtag #ClearTheLists. This moment not only helped teachers get supplies for their own classrooms, but it helped bring to light all the personal money teachers spend in their classrooms yearly.

It is worth the time to check out this great initiative that was ignited by teachers. It takes a lot more work, but the results could be worth it in the end. You may also want to tap into the parent-teacher association to help out, since you never know how they may be able to help until you ask. Remember it is only your first year, and your journey has just begun.

Teacher Expectation 4: Professional Workspace

So far, we have been talking about various expectations we have on certain components of teaching. We're sure that you have expectations of how your professional workplace will look and feel. For some, these expectations may be true. But what happens if it isn't quite what you had planned? What are your expectations for the workplace setting? Personalities? Support?

Expectations that don't hold true may not be completely terrible outcomes. As her intro states, Hannah S. spent four years learning the best educational practices in a self-contained classroom. Little did she know that she would not be teaching in that environment. Rather, Hannah has spent the past three years teaching one subject multiple times a day, and she loves it! Think about it friends, are you in the classroom in which you dreamed about during your first class, freshman year in college? Probably not. Do not be disappointed, though! It is a reality to have dreams, and sometimes those dreams play out differently . . . and might be better than you could have ever imagined! Dr. Sam shares,

> I went to college thinking I would be a first-grade teacher, thinking that was my dream job. I couldn't have been more wrong. My first teaching job was teaching middle school-aged students with multiple disabilities. I remember having a surreal out of body experience (yeah, it really felt like that). All eight students were in class alongside six adults (all older than me). I remember thinking to myself, "OK, where is the teacher? Oh, wait, it's me!" Put your hand up if you ever had that moment! As quickly as it came, it left, and I got into our lesson for the day. But I will never forget that moment of, *ok, where's the adult in the room?* And the realization that it was ME! If you have felt this way, you are not alone. I came to realize that teaching those eight students in a special education classroom was my dream job, and I loved it!"

[handwritten note: Wow! This was actually me! (just with 1 para)]

Make Magic Happen:

You may not end up in a location or teaching setting that you intended, and that is fine! Breathe—you've got this. Teaching is a journey, no matter the setting. Find a mentor where you are who can help you adjust.

Teacher Expectation 5: Supportive Administration

The longer you teach, the more you will learn about the importance of having the support of your administration. Let's get a little technical here: a study conducted at Rutgers University by Saul Rubinstein and John McCarthy showed that when educators and administration work together and alongside one another, student achievement will improve (Teachers Unions and Management Partnerships, 2014). At the end of the day, student success is everyone's main goal in education. When you are interviewing to find a job in an unfamiliar district or area, you need to realize that you are also interviewing the administrator. Is this person going to support you as a new teacher? → sometimes you don't have the luxury of choice of jobs

Abby M. shares how she learned to communicate effectively with her administrative team:

> I've learned a lot about working with administration in my first three years of teaching. In my experience, there has been a big push to hide behind the union when you have concerns or complaints. I constantly hear educators talking about bringing issues to the union for them to bring to our administrators. In my three years in education, my administrators have always appreciated and respected me for bringing my concerns directly to them. I've been in two different buildings with two different administrative teams, and I've never had a bad experience sharing a concern with them.
>
> One time I found myself very frustrated by a lapse in communication between my administrator and me. Long story short, I was struggling to get information that I needed about a significant change to my classroom, and I was feeling disrespected and unappreciated. Weeks after the change went into effect, I was still holding onto anger and frustration regarding this incident, and it wasn't until a very wise coworker and friend called me out for my bitterness that I realized I needed to do something about it. He encouraged me to talk with the administrators directly about my frustrations. Sweaty and nervous, I walked

into my principal's office and had an open but respectful conversation about my frustrations with them. Both administrators were incredibly appreciative and understanding of my concerns. This conversation helped build mutual trust and respect because we were able to have the 'what we can all do next time' conversation, and because it fostered a sense of teamwork and honesty. Avoid falling into the mentality of 'us vs. them' with administration. Yes, they are our bosses, but they have the same goal we do: to help kids."

Hannah T. learned this lesson as well. After being put on an improvement plan, she learned to view any sort of oversight as a bonus and a form of support. But it took some adjustment and a mindset shift-which was easier some days than others. Viewing it as a helping hand rather than a disciplinary action will make all the difference in your attitude and what you will get out of your time of 'improvement.'

We all need to be getting better, and improvement plans or similar things simply provide you with the resources and oversight to help you be better at the things you didn't even know you were struggling with. Being able to talk with your administrator, having access to additional professional development, and being told to take advantage of resources in your very own building is a great gift. Knowing that you all are there for the good of the kids can help you realize that you are all working toward the same goal, even if it is in different ways. Ultimately Hannah T. did not stay at her school, but rather than see it as a teaching failure, she saw that maybe that school was not a good fit for her at that point in her life. She took all that she had learned from her experiences, resources, and mentorship at that school and carried it with her to grow.

Abby T. makes a great point about why having a positive relationship with your administration is so important:

"   Having a good relationship with administration is so important. I have learned to ask questions when I don't understand something and to never complain about their decisions because *one day that might be you . . . in their shoes making those decisions.*"

Teacher Expectation 6 - Mentor Teacher

While it is definitely important to have a more experienced teacher to turn to, sometimes the one who is most helpful to you won't be the mentor assigned to you . . . or even a person in your building! Hannah T. depended a lot on her Twitter community for support and encouragement through a hard first year, and it was always helpful to have an outside perspective. In the building, sometimes the one who can be most specifically helpful to you is someone who is in your classroom regularly or who interacts with your students a lot. Asking for help in solving a specific challenge with a specific student is more helpful when you can talk with someone who knows the student.

In some schools, especially those with high turnover rates among the faculty, 'experienced' teacher is a relative term. Your mentor teacher may be a third- or fifth-year teacher. They certainly have more experience than you, and in some ways can be more understanding or sympathetic to your first-year struggles, since they were there not that long ago. However, they won't have the long-term perspective that a 10-, 15-, or 20-year veteran teacher would bring to the table. Being assigned a mentor teacher is a great starting point, but remember that YOU are in charge of finding answers to your questions and seeking advice. If one mentor can't help you, then widen your circle of mentors. No one ever said there could only be one!

Expectations as a Teacher

Every day, every moment, you are teaching your students. You might not feel that way after a unit test with a 60% pass rate, or when you read the exit slips after a lesson you thought was amazing, but clearly, your students didn't understand; however, your students are learning more from you than just reading, writing, and math. Hannah T. really struggled with this throughout the school year as her academic results were not always up to others' standards. She shares her experience as she realized this:

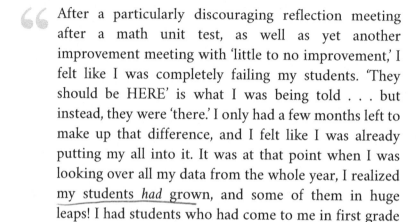
After a particularly discouraging reflection meeting after a math unit test, as well as yet another improvement meeting with 'little to no improvement,' I felt like I was completely failing my students. 'They should be HERE' is what I was being told . . . but instead, they were 'there.' I only had a few months left to make up that difference, and I felt like I was already putting my all into it. It was at that point when I was looking over all my data from the whole year, I realized my students *had* grown, and some of them in huge leaps! I had students who had come to me in first grade with a Pre-K reading level . . . and now they could read simple books! They may not have been on grade level for first grade, but they had progressed a year or more from where they had started!

Other teachers in my grade, more experienced teachers, had grown students more than that, but for me, I needed to see what I *had* done rather than what I *hadn't*. Ultimately, I started the year with only one student reading on grade level, but ended the year with at least eight, and ALL students had grown with some level of significance. Of course, my perfect wish, my expectation for myself, had been for all students to be on grade level, but rather than see my whole year as a failure for not meeting my expectations, I turned it around to celebrate the successes I *did* make.

For example, the shy student who I never heard speak

in September, was starting to grow as a leader by May. The girl who would put herself down whenever she struggled with something was beginning to have strategies to work through a problem and have confidence in academics. The girl who always followed her friends even when it wasn't a good choice was choosing to stand up for herself and help her friends make better choices. A gifted student realized that intelligence isn't just the ability to do hard math and that others were equally as intelligent. These were the non-academic successes I saw, and those are the ones that will hopefully stay with my students long after they can read."

Success for your students can take many different forms. Academic success is important, of course, but when you feel discouraged in one area, try to encourage yourself in another area before returning to what you struggle with. When you can tackle a problem, you have the confidence of having succeeded in something else, your whole outlook will change, and your students will ultimately benefit.

Make Magic Happen:

It's not a bad thing to have expectations for yourself or your students. You need clear goals that you can work towards as a team. But don't *just* look ahead at your goals; be sure to take the time to look back at your accomplishments, no matter what form they may take.

Expectations as a Leader

Friends, have you thought about your expectations as a leader? What makes a strong leader? Do you feel intimidated by being a leader as a new teacher? Do you feel that your experiences as a preservice teacher will allow you to be a leader? What experiences do you have in leadership roles that will carry over in the educational realm? What even IS a leader?! Don't be shy, let's list them out!

- assertive
- courageous
- friendly
- well-informed
- bold
- caring
- listener

Those roles, regardless if they have been in an educational setting or not, can help shape you for the job search journey and for the first year of teaching. Hannah S. got involved with EdCamps, organized the first #EdCampGCC, presented at conferences, and networked with her PLN—all while in college. So, when attending conferences as a beginning teacher, Hannah felt like she wasn't actually a newbie. She reflects and shares in her own words,

> Part of my preparedness was the initiative on my part that I took during my college years. I stepped up to the plate to become involved in a professional community and conferences while being a pre-service teacher. If I hadn't, I might not have felt as prepared for the job search, for interviews, or for connecting with administration. Sam was part of the fire for professional development (#eduawesome and #teachershoutout!) that was first ignited during college."

Now, we will tell you that there will be days that you are being a leader but feel a bit underqualified because you are a new teacher. However, embrace that newness! Who said that you had to be a veteran teacher to be a leader? So what if you weren't a leader in college? It's simple. Take initiative. As Gandalf states, "It's a dangerous business, Frodo, going out your door. You step onto the road, and if you don't keep your feet, there's no knowing where you might be swept off to." (Tolkien, 1954). It can be quite the journey once you take initiative, but be careful. Don't start jumping on every opportunity to be involved and have a leadership role that you are so engulfed in everything that you can't do one thing to the best of your ability.

Our suggestion is to start small. Is there an afterschool program where you can volunteer your time? Can you help plan a teacher-led in-service day? Can you attend a small-scale conference and bring back knowledge to your colleagues? Often, districts will ask teachers to sit on panels or committees and attend various day conferences. Volunteer for one of those opportunities. Is there an opportunity to be part of the planning for a local EdCamp or conference? If you don't know what leadership opportunities are available for you, seek them out. As a new teacher, you have a unique perspective to bring to the table in leadership roles. Take advantage of that ability.

Before we move on, please take a moment to write two goals for fulfilling leadership roles this upcoming school year. We challenge you to do this every year. Being a professional of impact means being involved. How can you be involved and lead?

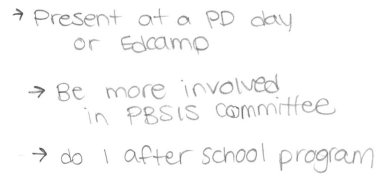

→ Present at a PD day
   or Edcamp

→ Be more involved
   in PBSIS committee

→ do 1 after school program

1.

(goals listed
on previous
page)

2.

Expectations as a Learner

While there may be many professional development (PD) opportunities that sound interesting to you, make sure that you are getting the most out of your valuable time. Be certain that the one you choose is one that will apply to you and will provide you with inspiration and ideas you will be able to start utilizing right away. Get what YOU need out of your PD! Professional development is one requirement that is needed for all educators, from preservice to veteran- we can all do better and be better for our students.

As you grow as a teacher, you will notice that there are many opportunities for you to learn and expand on what you know. Some professional development opportunities are provided by the district in which you work and most likely are required. Some professional development sessions provided by the district are very helpful and informative- others not so much. So, how does an edumagician approach this? Well, friends, we want you to take back your PD- own it! After all, it is YOUR professional development. Remember- just like in college, don't go to PD for the A or for the credit. Go for the learning. It is going to help you grow and shape you as an educator if you focus on the learning outcomes instead of a grade or how many hours you will get in the end. Those things are important, but they are not the end-all, be-all. OK, are you ready for some great ways to own your own professional development? Buckle up- here we go!

- Twitter chats: Any time of any day or night, they last from 15 minutes to one hour on every educational topic imaginable. Hop on the calendar and find the one that works for you and speaks to your teaching heart. We recommend for new   · teachers- #NTchat and New Teachers to Twitter #NT2t.

Education Twitter Chats Calendar

- Voxer chats: Voxer is a walkie talkie app that people use to connect using voice memos and text. Dr. Sam shares that she uses Voxer to communicate with fellow authors, and that she participated and even led a session during EdCamp Voice using Voxer. There are also book chats that occur using Voxer.

Voxer EdChats

- Edcamps: Edcamps are unconferences—meaning the sessions are not planned until the day of the conference. Participants come to camp with ideas of topics that they would like to learn more about. These ideas get written on a sticky note, and the session board is built by the ideas of the participants. Edcamps are discussion-based, meaning there are no formally led presentations. Edcamps are built upon the idea that the smartest person in the room IS the room. Everyone can learn and lead together.

Edcamp Website

- Webinars: Participate in a webinar on your own time. One of our go-to resources for webinars is Simple K12. They have webinars on a variety of topics for teachers led by leaders in the field. Whether you attend live or watch a recorded webinar, there is a lot to learn online.

- Podcasts: Podcasts are PD in your PJs or in your car. These are amazing resources for teachers, by teachers. Topics can range from content specific to educational technology tools to best practices.

Make Magic Happen:

In the blank space, write three ways that you can own your PD this school year. Find the resources to support YOU as a teacher—own it!

We talked about expectations as a teacher, leader, and learner. These expectations were influenced by your years as a preservice teacher. College prepared you to teach, but with practice, you will perfect your craft. Let's flip the script here and take some time to chat about what college may not have prepared you for when it came to teaching.

What did your college experience NOT prepare you for?

As a professor in higher education, Dr. Sam shares, "We try to prepare our future teachers as much as we can, so they can become educators of excellence. However, there is no way we can prepare them for every 'what if' situation that can happen to new teachers." The first year of teaching can feel like a whirlwind of emotion. You will have many moments where you may feel, "Wow, I wasn't expecting that." Madison B. has a great metaphor to describe college versus the first year of teaching:

 If you look at your teaching career as a whole house, I initially believed that college would build the foundation, walls, and roof. All that I would have to do, as a teacher, would be to paint the walls and decorate the house. In reality, college created a really solid foundation. The first year of teaching built the walls, and the journey continues. Teaching (especially at the beginning) is a slow grow. Rest assured, college taught me how to learn; how to fail and grow from it."

So get ready as we dive into just a couple things that college may not have prepared you for!

Emotional Baggage

We know that college can't prepare you for the emotional roller-coaster that teaching takes you on. But you will survive it. You will be that kid that gets off the roller coaster and says, "Let's do it again!" and you will run to get back in line. Hannah S. shares,

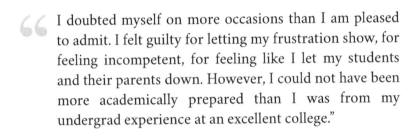

> I doubted myself on more occasions than I am pleased to admit. I felt guilty for letting my frustration show, for feeling incompetent, for feeling like I let my students and their parents down. However, I could not have been more academically prepared than I was from my undergrad experience at an excellent college."

College gave Hannah the tools needed to prepare for the hardships and disappointments that come with teaching (we will explore these in Chapters 2 and 3). When pondering what college didn't prepare her for, Hannah quickly answers: baggage. The hardest things for her to manage were the difficulties that she saw students struggling through. The following is an excerpt from a presentation Hannah S. gave to pre-service teachers about the life of a first-year teacher:

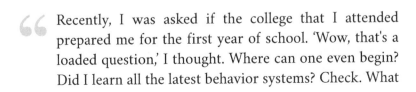

> Recently, I was asked if the college that I attended prepared me for the first year of school. 'Wow, that's a loaded question,' I thought. Where can one even begin? Did I learn all the latest behavior systems? Check. What

about the importance of parent communication? Check. Planning and preparation? Check. All of the components of Danielson? Check. I was handed all of the tools one might think is needed . . . until I learned that that was just the tip of the iceberg. No one really understands, nor can comprehend what it is like to be a teacher. The first half of the year was a blur. I know that I wasn't the teacher that I prepared for four years to become. I know that I failed my students. I know that I let parents down. But I also know that I learned, I grew, and I became a better person. The "whirlwind" slump was over. Christmas break came at a much-needed time for me.

I came back from Christmas break refreshed and with a new attitude. The overflowing workload . . . fine. The lesson planning . . . that's not new. The grading . . . it'll get faster with time. The baggage . . . I wasn't ready. My heart breaks. But every single day, my heart is overflowing with kids that bring a smile to my face, that challenge me, that love me, that teach me. I'm far from perfect, but I pray that I can be the perfect thing for these kids. Don't lose hope, my friends." (Sansom, 2017)

Learning how to manage the emotional rollercoaster is one aspect of teaching you can't fully prepare for via college courses, and we will talk about this baggage in the next two chapters. But friends, remember that you are Edumagicians! You are in that room for a reason! When things get emotionally taxing, remember your WHY and turn to Chapter 7 for some inspiration.

Differentiation. . . IRL

On the other hand, an area that we cover in college a lot is . . . drum roll . . . differentiating instruction for our students. We talk about it

TO DEATH in college. It is both something you are very prepared for and something you can never be prepared for. As we wrote this chapter, Hannah T. mentioned, "I feel like if you space out in class and you are called on by the professor to answer a question, you can just say 'differentiation' and you are right." Honestly, you can do case studies, but what can *really* prepare you for differentiation other than actually differentiating for real students? Yes, it's something that you should know exists, that it's important, and some of the basic and general ways to do it. But being able to differentiate for your specific classroom is something you can't do to the fullest until you know your students well.

Friends, it doesn't make you a failure if you aren't meeting the individual needs of every student you teach by the end of September. Now, if it is April and you aren't meeting needs, then we need to have a different conversation. Use time with your learners to gather information about each of them, finding common denominators among them when it comes to learning styles and methods. Start to introduce broad examples of differentiation . . . auditory vs. visual vs. kinesthetic, for example. From there, you can gather more information. Don't forget to reflect, reflect, reflect! What is working? What isn't? Are there some students that are still not quite being reached? Observe them more . . . what do they need? Differentiation is such an ongoing process of trial and error, and the errors are important to refine our technique. Don't let perfection be the enemy of progress! Make a change and see how it goes. What are some small changes you can implement right away? What needs would they meet?

When we are reflective, we can help our learners move forward, we can find and diagnose misconceptions, and we can help guide our learners' thinking along the right path. We become intentional with our decisions. We reflect and start to see our learners as individuals. You start to ask yourself how you can scaffold and grow individual students. When we reflect, we ask how we can better reach and support our learners.

Strengths of Learner	Needs of Learner	Differentiation Technique to Reach Learner

Your professors and the experiences that they set up for you as pre-service teachers are specifically designed to help you learn to be on the other side of the desk as a teacher. Moreover, you are able to learn the best practices and techniques for teaching x, y, and z. Friends, college won't prepare you for all of it. You will grow- you may not feel it, but each day, you will! Use what you were given and run with it! You've got this!

```
┌─────────────────────────────────────────────────┐
│                                                   │
│                        2                          │
│                                                   │
│        D: Dealing with Disappointment             │
│                                                   │
└─────────────────────────────────────────────────┘
```

DISAPPOINTMENT. Maybe that's a word you don't want to think about as you are starting the "honeymoon" phase of a new job, but we want to be real and honest. As with anything, disappointments will come. This chapter is simply a "survival guide" per se, not something intended to intimidate you or cause worry. Disappointments, as you are aware, are part of life, and it's OK. We want to prepare you to be an educator of excellence, and sometimes disappointment is a pit stop. Just a pit stop. Pit stops are meant for a quick visit, not a long stay, but are still part of the journey. Visit it, don't stay long, and know that we all go (and grow) through it.

During this part, we are going to share some areas of disappointment-pit stops that we encountered during the first few years of teaching. It is going to be honest, raw reflection. Think of it as a way to prepare for things that can/will arise. But don't worry, friends, you are going to get through this and even be better off for having gone through it! Keep that in mind as we share our hearts with you. OK, deep breath-here we go. These are in no particular order.

Pit Stop 1: Not-So-Pinterest-Perfect Classroom

We are pretty positive that you have that one board on Pinterest where you have pinned all the greatest organizational hacks and color schemes for the best classroom ever. Sure, you have a dream of what it will look like, but remember, it all may not come together just so. It can be overwhelming to decide where to begin. Sometimes you can get access to your classroom a month in advance; in other cases, you get the keys to your classroom one week before school starts or less! You may not have the resources, budget, or space to do all of the wonderfully creative things that you had planned. If that is something you are struggling with, read on!

Hannah T. started off her first year of teaching in a new state, new school, and on one leg (she was on crutches)! She shares that starting in a room on crutches puts a damper on classroom arrangement, but more importantly,

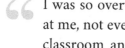

> I was so overwhelmed with all the information coming at me, not even knowing how to go about setting up my classroom and not being able to do anything quickly before moving on to the next thing. I ended up finding unimportant tasks I could do while sitting in one place. In the end, my room was the bare minimum when students walked through the door . . . not exactly what I had envisioned for my bright new school year."

It is OK—in fact, it is more than OK if your classroom is not Pinterest-perfect. You don't want it to be too busy or cluttered. Most importantly, it is not only YOUR classroom, but it is also your students' classroom. Get their input on design, layout, etc. Hannah T. goes onto say, "Yeah, it was never the Pinterest room I had envisioned in my student teaching days, but it was a place where students learned and grew, knew what was expected of them, and even knew where things belonged!" Isn't that what we all want anyway—somewhere our students can learn, lead, and grow? Somewhere that they come in excited to learn and collaborate? Somewhere all of our students can be accepted for who they are? YES! Friends, all of that doesn't come from Pinterest or the Target dollar spot- it comes from you and your heart.

Make Magic Happen:

Want to organize your classroom without all the heavy lifting? Try designing it in FloorPlanner first!

FloorPlanner

Hannah S. doesn't personally use FloorPlanner. Instead, she draws her plans out on paper at the end of the previous year, allowing time to adjust as she thinks of things over the summer and during the initial setup in August. She also plans her bulletin boards ahead of time and has gone as far as getting things up and covered for the following year. She keeps most of the boards the same throughout the year (number lines, math talk stems, and math tools) but changes one as she progresses through units. Ultimately, the setup comes down to you. Are you an online planner, or do you prefer paper and pen? What works best for you? Hannah S. switched her layout several times until she found the one that worked the best for her and the atmosphere of her classroom. Have a plan (we will talk more about this in Chapter G) but recognize that you may need to adjust your dream designs.

Pit Stop 2: Failure

We all know that failure is going to happen, but it is one of those things that we don't really think of until it does. Hannah T. recalls a time when she was doing guided reading with her little learners. She shares:

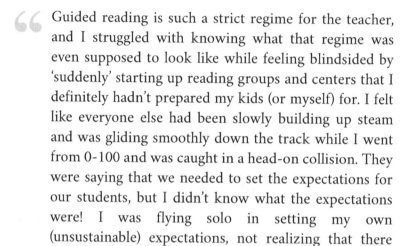 Guided reading is such a strict regime for the teacher, and I struggled with knowing what that regime was even supposed to look like while feeling blindsided by 'suddenly' starting up reading groups and centers that I definitely hadn't prepared my kids (or myself) for. I felt like everyone else had been slowly building up steam and was gliding smoothly down the track while I went from 0-100 and was caught in a head-on collision. They were saying that we needed to set the expectations for our students, but I didn't know what the expectations were! I was flying solo in setting my own (unsustainable) expectations, not realizing that there was a group standard I would be held to. It took me ALL YEAR to recover from this costly mistake, ultimately leading to me leaving my school.

In hindsight, I could have asked around about what was coming up, what I should be doing during that reading time, or even asked to observe another class. I should have been more vulnerable and open from the start to ask for help. More situations were going on in my classroom and personal life that were also adding to the noise, so I didn't have the opportunity to stop and realize that I couldn't ask questions if I didn't know what to ask. You don't know what you don't know, and I thought that I knew."

Friends, learn from Hannah's lesson. That is why we are sharing these moments of growth with you. Sometimes you need to take a breath and pause, stop and think . . . what is coming up for my students? How can I best prepare them for this transition? If you are struggling with a certain area, ask a mentor or veteran teacher that you trust for support or to bounce ideas off of. Think about connecting with the teaching community online via Instagram or Twitter. Be honest with yourself and ask yourself, "What do I not know? Can I ask for clarification about anything I *think* I know?" Perhaps observe other classrooms to get an idea of what other teachers are doing to help inform your practice.

Make Magic Happen:

When you observe other teachers, go with a purpose. What area of classroom management, lesson delivery, closure, routine, transition, or behavior do you want to focus on during your observation? Be courteous of the other teacher's time. Ask him/her for a date and time that fits their schedule. Take notes as you observe to either remember things for yourself or ask questions about later.

Pit Stop 3: Self Disappointment

The next disappointment to discuss is one of the rawest, yet easiest to write because of self-criticism. One of the hardest things we can do to ourselves is to be critical. It is only natural that you may beat yourself up for a subpar lesson, or forgetting to contact a parent, or over/underreacting to a particular situation. First, don't feel guilty! Give yourself a break. The fact that you are being critical of yourself shows just how much you care about being the best educator you can possibly be! Second, like with any disappointment, self-disappointment is a pit stop that you are meant to move on from and learn from. Don't let it become a monster that brings you down and harms your self-esteem, dignity, and self-perception as an educator.

The most important thing to remember as you start this journey is that the first year (or few) is made up of live and learn experiences.

Hannah S. thinks back to her first year, which she describes as a whirlwind. There were times that she felt like she let her students and their parents down. She focused too much on her mistakes, not the lessons from those mistakes. During her first year, Hannah S. started to revamp her curriculum (which is always changing based on the unique learners), and with it came many trials and errors. She got a lot of activities from books and resources but also spent time making her own worksheets and tests. Somehow, she seemed to overlook spelling errors or minute details/directions. One day she assigned the wrong homework problems that left parents questioning. She felt small on those days. She felt imperfect, like a failure, and disappointed . . . like she let her students and their parents down. She felt incompetent, and thinks back to the day of bathroom tears:

 I lived and learned so much during the first year about so many different things. But I'll never forget the day that it felt like it was all coming crashing down. It was the first part of my first year, and I was teaching third-grade math in a departmentalized school. In other words, that meant I was a 22-year-old teacher feeling pressure for my students' success in mathematics since I was their sole math teacher in the tested subject area. I'm not going to sugar coat anything . . . the first year is hard! It's a huge, huge, HUGE learning curve.

I had just learned of a minor way in which I caused some frustration, but to me, it felt like I was being questioned in my competence as a teacher. Looking back, it was actually a minor comment that I should have brushed off. But it was the first comment that made me question my ability as a teacher, and it made me feel small. It was all I could do to get through the rest of the class, take my kiddos to lunch, sign a paper briefly in my principal's office, and make it back to my room without letting the flood gates open. My colleague/mentor/friend followed me and hugged me as I tried to not let the tears of frustration fall. I don't remember everything she said, but I do remember her comforting me and making me feel valued and worthy. I later went to the bathroom to let the tears fall and compose myself.

I let a mere comment break me down and get the best of me. You WILL make mistakes. You WILL mess up. It's part of figuring out the whole teaching thing. It's ok to have those moments when you just need to let it out. For me, it was getting a pep talk from a colleague, shedding a few tears with her, and composing myself in the bathroom. If you need to take a moment and let it out so you can get yourself together—do it. There will be days that you feel incompetent, but I think we all will have those days regardless of our title, our position, our rank, or our career. It's part of being human, but let me tell you something- do not give up on yourself! Have faith in you. You CAN and WILL succeed! It's all about learning from mistakes, having the wisdom to handle challenges, and growing and maturing as an educator. Live and learn. Find a way to let go and realize that you ARE competent. Believe in yourself."

Hannah S. also shares, "I can be a perfectionist but had to learn that it is ok to not be perfect!" Hear that?! It is OK to not be perfect. Reality check: You WON'T be, and you AREN'T perfect. Breathe. Use your moments of "failure" (which . . . friend . . . you aren't a failure) to learn and grow. Use mistakes and errors on papers as life lessons for your students, to show them that adults and teachers make mistakes. We learn from mistakes. There will be days when you feel as though your incompetencies outweigh your competencies. It's only when we don't grow from our mistakes and failures that we have *truly* failed.

EduMagicians, stand up tall, look yourself in the mirror, and strike the best superhero pose you can muster. Be determined. Tell yourself, "I can do this! I got this." This is called a power pose. Some of the authors got to practice this in one of their college classes (thank you, Tammi Martin), and while you may feel silly at first, it definitely helps you feel more confident as you go on to tackle any task! As mentioned previously, teaching is a 'live and learn' experience. You will feel a lack of confidence and question your competence. You will make mistakes, but hey, we all do! Have faith in yourself! You are educated. You were hired, showing that someone has faith in you. You were chosen for this field and for THIS job. You know what you are doing, even though it may feel otherwise.

 Make Magic Happen:

Keep something motivational, a picture or quote, on or near your desk to remind you that you can do this, that you are not a failure. Simple things such as a picture from a student or a motivational quote can truly boost your confidence. Have something handy for the days that you are hard on yourself.

Pit Stop 4: Mentor Teacher

We know you leave college thinking that you know everything there is to know about teaching. But you don't know what you don't know. It is true, right? Sometimes you don't know, and maybe your mentor teacher doesn't know the answer either. Hannah T. shares,

> My mentor was pretty good about checking in with me, especially at the beginning of the year and near progress reports and report cards. She really helped me to understand the logistics of how my school worked, but she wasn't always able to help me do better at the actual *teaching* part, mostly because what seemed like common sense to her at that point was something that I still needed to be spelled out for me."

Hannah T. didn't even know how to ask to do better. She didn't realize that she was drowning until she turned in her guided reading plans in November and was told that they were 'unacceptable.' Her mentor could only help her so much because the mentor had assumed that Hannah understood the basics of guided reading instruction. It isn't anyone's fault that she didn't know what she didn't know.

Friends, please take advantage of not just your mentor, but of all the other teachers on your team, and even in your wing, who may have more experience with teaching in general. Everyone has strengths, weaknesses, and wisdom, but sometimes, you may need to go find it. Is your mentor relationship rocky? That's OK because you can reach out to others. Don't only depend on your assigned mentor, branch out and talk to other teachers whether they are down the hall or online. Reach out to find your own learning and mentorship. Ask for help from others in your grade level or subject area, but also ask for general tips from the veteran teachers you can find in your school.

Make Magic Happen:

You don't know what you don't know, and your mentor may not either. So ask and keep asking questions. No question is too small. Ask for someone to look over your plans or to observe you teaching. It's OK to get feedback, positive and negative. In teaching, feedback should be welcomed, since we want to be the best we can be for our students. Getting feedback from others is key to improving ourselves!

Pit Stop 5: Not Reaching that ONE Student

Leaving college, you feel that you are going to make a connection with every student that walks through your door. You will do everything in your power to reach every child in your room. You probably will do it too. However, no matter what you do, there might be that child you cannot make a connection with. . . and Katy G. is here to tell you it is okay.

During Katy's first year of teaching, she had a student that posed some challenges in the classroom. We will call this student Colt. Katy used her time after school to read his file, walk him to class, attend his sporting events, and other ways that she found could help build rapport between them. She did everything right, she understood that building rapport with students is one of the best ways to reach them. But Colt continued to be disruptive in the classroom, unfocused on his academics, and was still getting into trouble. It broke Katy's heart because deep down, she knew he wanted to do the right thing. Katy and her team teacher worked together all year to help this student succeed. But despite their endless research, parent involvement, and trying to help him understand that his studies are very important, it did not seem to work. Colt continued to struggle academically and behaviorally the entire year. They even tried to get his coaches involved to improve his academics, but this did not help either. It was not that Katy and her team didn't try to reach this student or gave up; it just was not his time. To this day, no matter how challenging Colt is in the classroom, Katy always hopes for the best. She talked to his new teachers, and he seems to have improved in the new year. Maybe you are experiencing something similar in your teaching. Friends know that you are not alone. Shayla S. shares a similar story of a student that she worked so hard to reach:

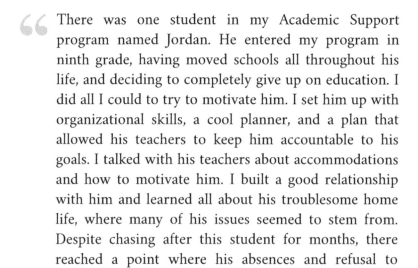

There was one student in my Academic Support program named Jordan. He entered my program in ninth grade, having moved schools all throughout his life, and deciding to completely give up on education. I did all I could to try to motivate him. I set him up with organizational skills, a cool planner, and a plan that allowed his teachers to keep him accountable to his goals. I talked with his teachers about accommodations and how to motivate him. I built a good relationship with him and learned all about his troublesome home life, where many of his issues seemed to stem from. Despite chasing after this student for months, there reached a point where his absences and refusal to complete assignments were too stacked against him. He opened up about psychological issues our school wasn't equipped to assist with. Some of his teachers weren't accommodating and had given up on him. Things looked hopeless for this student who was sucking away teacher effort and still flunking all his classes. His mom was at a loss and couldn't follow through with the advice we had given her. So even though I had spent a significant amount of time investing in Jordan, I was part of the teacher committee that decided to expel him. I had to admit that my school, and I myself did not have the resources to help him. I felt like I failed him, and I wondered if I did enough. I knew he didn't have a better school to go to in the developing country we were living in.

I eventually came to the point where I had to admit that we did all we could to help him succeed, and it wasn't enough to reach him. I had to detach myself from the situation a bit and put up a boundary. I learned that there will be some cases that I just can't beat, and some kids that I just won't be able to reach, for reasons outside of my control. That doesn't mean the effort is wasted, though. Every kid deserves to have a teacher fighting for them, even if it's not enough."

What a story! Katy G. and Shayla S. both learned the value of fighting for a student and putting in their best effort to help that student succeed. It is tempting to see it as a failure when a student doesn't grow with all of our best efforts, but we need to remind ourselves that we can't know the long-term impact that our dedication may have in that student's life. Maybe many years down the road, they will remember that teacher who worked so hard for them and believed in them, and they will start to believe in themselves for the first time. You may never know if your efforts paid off. But it should not matter because it is not about you! It is about these students who have so much going on in their personal lives that they need a cheerleader. Even if it seems your efforts are not paying off, never give up on any child, no matter how challenging. Just like Shayla said, "Every kid deserves to have a teacher fighting for them, even if it's not enough."

Make Magic Happen:

Even though Katy and Shayla did not see the results they hoped to see in their students, it did not mean they did not gain anything. You will have students that you desperately want to succeed, and for them to stop being their own roadblocks in their learning. But unfortunately, you might not be that person to make it happen. But that does not mean you should stop trying to reach that child.

Pulling Away from the Pit Stop

We know that our disappointments were raw and honest. One way to really help you work through and overcome your disappointments is through reflecting. We left space at the end of the book for reflections- use it! If the purpose of a pit stop is to tune up a car, the purpose of going through disappointment and failure is to tune up your teaching.

Any educator will tell you how important it is to be reflective, and it's often part of how you will be scored on an evaluation as a teacher of tenure. It can help you consider that outside perspective, the view that you can only get when you take a step back. Edumagicians, here are a few tips on reflection that we have for you.

- Identify Positives: When it comes to reflecting on a lesson, identify two positives (something has to go right in the lesson, right?) and one thing that can be improved upon next time you teach that lesson. Write them on your lesson plan or during your lesson planning include a table so you can easily reflect.

Positive 1: Student focus Positive students took away? Engagement strategy/hook?	Positive 2: Teacher focus Your delivery, closure, anticipatory set, transition, etc.	1 area that I would change next time I teach this lesson or topic.

- Journal: Hannah S. swears that every new teacher needs a reflective journal of the "Do's" and "Don'ts" you learn during the first year of teaching. Anyhow, she kept a journal where she would make notes on each unit commenting on what to change or what to keep for next year. This was extremely beneficial because the first year is a whirlwind, and you will forget things by the time you plan that same unit in twelve short months. On a personal note, it is fun to look back at the funny comments or try to decipher what that quick, abbreviated note was.

- Checklists: On a professional note, Hannah S. keeps a current record of which students need reteaching after a specific skill, required enrichment, or simply are on track and needed more support. She shares one idea that she adopted from her Dos and Don'ts reflection was to adapt her gradebook into a skills checklist per unit. For each skill, the student earned a "+" or "-" to indicate whether or not the student had mastered that specific skill set. She explains, she gave a pretest and indicated where each student was based on the results of the pre-test. Then, after the first quiz on the first skill, she went back and indicated which students did not yet master the first skill and which need enrichment. For the students that showed mastery based on the results of a pre-test, these students would be guided in more enriched or faster-paced learning to review the skills they know, and to enrich these skills for higher-order thinking that the other learners were not ready for. When this becomes more demanding (because of the large number of students), Hannah relies on simple reflective notes from her flexible groups.

Make Magic Happen:

By being intentional with record-keeping, Hannah S. was able to keep up with grades and feedback promptly and give her students the tailored instruction that they need. Friends, it does take time to carefully monitor. But once you have a system of monitoring learning and using current data, you will be able to quickly create flexible groups to better support your learners. After all, isn't that what we want- a classroom of learners who are excited, challenged, and supported? Oh YEAH!

3

U: Unstoppable

THERE WILL BE days in teaching that bring you such tremendous joy that your face will hurt from smiling so much. Days when a child 'gets it,' and you can see that lightbulb moment happen. Days where you get a hand-drawn picture, card, or gift for no other reason than just because. Or days, when a child looks up at you, beaming and says, "you are the best teacher since sliced bread (or Pokémon or fidget spinners—whatever is on-trend)." But there will be other days that bring you overwhelming sadness—a sadness so deep that it brings you to your knees.

This chapter was the most difficult to write and work through. It deals with some heavy topics, but we want to be able to share our experiences with you even when they are hard so that you can know that you are not alone. You may never go through these experiences, you may go through some, or you may go through different but equally difficult ones. No matter what you may face, you MUST remind yourself that you are unstoppable. Unstoppable at reaching every child. Unstoppable at loving. Unstoppable at doing your best to close language barriers. Unstoppable.

Unstoppable Student Events

Loss of a student

When you teach, we know it's not just us in the classroom. We teach people- we teach learners. We form relationships with our students, and we get to know them as people. They become our family. We once heard a new teacher share, "my class of eight students wasn't a class, we were a family." Just like a family, you celebrate the highs and the lows that happen, and you work through them together, as a team, as a family. Dr. Sam shares a story that happened early in her teaching career:

 On a hot sunny day in June, I was heading back from a day at the lake with family. I was in a place with limited cell service (hey it was the early 2000's), and when we got into a spot where we got service, my phone started to ding, buzz, and light up with messages. They were text messages and voice memos from my coworkers. My heart sank. . . I knew something must have happened to one of our students. The students in my class had many needs, and some were medically fragile. I was beginning my second year teaching and with one year under my belt, I was excited about new beginnings. My class had some of the same students in it from last year, as I was teaching special education pull-out class, and I had students several years in a row. I felt as a team we were getting in a groove together, and the students were making progress with their yearly goals. Nothing could have prepared me for the voice messages I received from my classroom assistant, parent of the child, personal care aides, all pretty much saying the same thing: 'Sam, call me. It's an emergency.'

I called my classroom assistant, and she shared that one of our students passed away in his sleep the night before. I remember my ears feeling heavy and deafening; I couldn't believe what she said. I later learned how he passed, when the services were, etc. After crying in the car, I regained some composure and called the parent. She answered right away- we cried together, we shared favorite memories, and at the end of the conversation, I knew what I could do to help. I created a memorial video with all of his favorite songs and pictures from friends and family. With a few days turn around, I created a video that honored his memory.

Needless to say, the school year started with a small dark cloud, but as the year progressed, we thought of ways we could remember and honor the student. His parents donated all of the assistive technology they had in the home to the school, and we created a lending library in his honor. That way, all students could try out some assistive technology and listen to some of his favorite books on tape."

In a moment where Dr. Sam felt helpless, she found that she could contribute to her student's memory by creating a memorial video. Friends, if you find yourselves in a similar situation and you are feeling overwhelmed with the loss of a student, please seek out help. Talk to a counselor or therapist, journal, create a way that you can honor the student. To be honest, she has a framed photo of the student in her office today to keep his memory alive.

Challenges at Home

Another sad reality to teaching is all your students' families will not look or be set up the same. Some will be better off, have both parents in the picture, parents separated, families that live in different states or countries, and even deceased parents. Please keep this in mind when starting the year. No one has a perfect family, even if they try to portray it. One teacher shares the following story about a student:

 Caleb was the jokester, knew all his current events, and told it how it was but was still respectful. He also enjoyed the outdoors, small talk, and watching basketball. With all these fantastic qualities, he tried to put on a face that he had it all going on and didn't need any help, which caused him to be a wallflower in some classrooms. I made it a point to greet the students each morning and try to do some check-ins with each child. Especially with how their homework went the night before, and if they needed any assistance. We had just finished covering integers, and Caleb was really struggling with it. What I soon found out was that he was a perfectionist. He did not believe that learning a new concept sometimes takes time, he felt he needed to be able to do it right the first time. My efforts to teach him to have a growth mindset instead of a fixed one made no matter.

What I failed to mention about this child thus far is he lost his mother from an overdose. He had been with her when it occurred. His father was not a very good role model and was in jail. Therefore, he was living with his grandparents. He had a lot of fear of being like his parents. Holidays were very tough for him because his peers would talk about all the great memories they were making with their parents. Between academics and socialization, it was very tough on him, and he did not want to discuss it with anyone. He already had the mindset that he needed to solve all his challenges on his own. I had to call down to the guidance counselor on multiple occasions because he would not make the appointment himself."

To be a child and to experience more tragedy than most adults do in their entire life is hard to imagine. Most teachers, though not all, have not even come close to understanding the home experiences their students come from every day. However, it is good to continue to remind ourselves to be patient with these children. We do not lower our expectations, but still, give them grace when it is needed. These children will thrive more in an environment where they feel that they belong, and they are safe. If they do not have these basic needs met in the classroom, they will shut down because they will think you're just like anyone else in their life that might have disappointed them.

As a new teacher, be ready to listen and not talk. These students that have very sad stories sometimes just need an adult to listen to them instead of talking at them. Never pretend to think you know what they are going through unless you have personally experienced it yourself. Even if you can share a similar experience with a student, be mindful that every person handles things differently. Be there and be a support for them. Talk to your school counselor for strategies of how to listen to students when they share hard things with you. These students will learn more from you academically if you invest in building this bridge with them first.

Mental Health

Students of all ages can struggle with things that we are in no way equipped to deal with. Another teacher shares her experience with a student struggling with suicidal thoughts:

 Kacey was the class clown of the room but was very intelligent. However, Kacey did not always want to show her classmates how knowledgeable she actually was in the classroom. She was almost four grade levels above for her reading level, but you would never know it. Kacey also had a very unfortunate family situation. When she was younger, her biological parents dropped her off at the babysitter's but never returned. Her biological parents got involved with drugs. The babysitter ended up adopting her and her younger brother.

The year I taught Kacey, her biological mother came back into the picture but did not have custody of her. The mother was in a relationship with new children of her own. The adoptive mother had her first biological grandbaby on the way and, therefore, wanted to be there for when the child was born and to help take care of him/her. The adoptive mother left Kacey and her brother with another babysitter for the entire quarter. During this quarter, Kacey's grades dropped, she wore the same clothes, did not have a bedtime, and was very confused about this situation. This led to Kacey writing a suicide note in my classroom. I watched her write it! I grabbed the notebook originally thinking she was trying to be funny about something in math- later to read lines (of a three-page paper), that she could not believe she 'would be dead at the age of ten.' My heart broke, and I immediately contacted the office without her noticing.

The office contacted the adoptive mother, who was still not home with the children. The principal told the parent about the situation. As a teacher, I would have thought that this mother would have been grateful to the teacher catching this note before something serious happened. Instead, she told the principal, she didn't write it.' The principal explained that I had seen Kacey write it in the middle of class. The mom was in denial. On the bright side, the mother was okay with Kacey signing up for counseling at the school.

After this incident, I made it a point to try to support

Kacey as much as possible. I had personally just lost a very close friend the prior year to suicide. I found as many resources as possible. I decided to use the daily journal technique. I provided Kacey with a journal and told her whenever she has questions or when she feels like no one is listening. . . write it down. Then she can hand it to me, and I will return it to her. I told her I would not judge. I added that she can write in it whenever and there is no timeline.

Kacey used the notebook from time to time, but nothing ever as serious as the day I found the letter came up. I tell you this story to remind you of the importance of building rapport with your students. I would have never known about that letter unless I knew Kacey's normal habits. As I stated previously, Kacey was my happy go lucky student and was always cracking a joke. Never would I have expected that from her. The family situation she was dealing with really affected her academics. But I wouldn't have been able to help her unless I understood and listened. I might not always have the correct answer or have experienced similar situations. But I can always provide empathy and try to understand."

What a sobering story. We are the first line of defense in helping our students, but when we feel out of our depth or unsure about something, it is important to take it to those more qualified to help our kids. We can ask for help for ourselves, too, advice on how to monitor students, see red flags, and intervene in safe and effective ways. After this situation, the teacher got help for themselves by talking to coworkers and counselors to debrief and process the situation. This teacher also did a great job of creating a safe place for Kacey to seek help and support in the form of a notebook. Friends, it is so important to build a space where students feel safe, valued, and secure. What are the ways that you can create safe spaces for students in your class-room? Take time to jot down some ideas below.

Teaching can be an emotional rollercoaster. It can be taxing, frustrating, saddening. We look into their little eyes, and we wish we could change their home life. Hannah S. shares,

> I used to say that I had six hours to help change a child's life. Now, I have sixty minutes. I give them the best I can and pray for God to do the rest. I know that I have made mistakes. I know that I have gotten it wrong. I know that I didn't handle that situation right. I know that I am not a perfect teacher. Many days, I leave school feeling inadequate. Being a teacher makes you feel mother-like. I find myself calling them "mine" and "my kids," knowing full well that they are simply my students.
>
> I wish that I could sincerely call them my own and that I could provide for them as my parents did. I feel

inadequate because I am not able to provide for their every need. I feel inadequate because there are just so many situations that I cannot intervene in. They are too young and too innocent to see and experience what they do. Education is just a mere fraction of the needs that children have" (Sansom, 2016).

Maybe you look at the little girl in your class wearing the same jacket all week and make a wish that you could give her a new one. You look at them all and wish a special wish for each of your students. Maybe you say a simple wish for yourself:

"I wish that I could get it right the first time. . . all of the time. I wish that it would have been a prior thought, not an afterthought. I wish that there were more hours in the day. I wish that I didn't feel guilty about going to bed, knowing that there is still more to do."

Surround yourself with teacher friends who understand the trials of teaching. Find a support system. Love on the kids, even in your darkest moments. You may let your guard down and get frustrated, but remember, "they aren't giving you a hard time, they are having a hard time." This may be true more than we realize.

Unstoppable Communication

Navigating Language Barriers

Communicating with parents is definitely a huge part of being a teacher. In many ways, parents and teachers are co-teachers in a student's life and education. So, what do you do when there is a language barrier between you and the parent? If you have a high ESOL population, your school will make sure that official things are available in multiple languages, but what about those phone calls home (good or not), weekly newsletters, quick notes, or corrections on work sent home? Hannah T. had a solid majority of students whose parents didn't speak English, and it was a weekly challenge of how to communicate positive and negative news to parents when needed- not to mention wrangling permission slips! A lot of mistakes, planning, and making friends with multiple translators were what finally carried her to the end of the school year.

Conferences become extra important in these instances when you know you'll have a translator, so make sure you are very prepared and ready to talk about any sort of communication system you want to use with the parent going forward (like sticker or smiley charts). Making sure that parents know you are on their side, and you are both a team will go a long way in teaching their child.

ClassDojo's 'story' feature also has a translate button! Parents can get a rough translation of what you post, so sharing positive things that way is simple. Other communication technologies often have translate features as well. When using these, keep in mind that the translation will only be so good. Be sure to use simple sentences and words so that a general meaning can be conveyed through a basic translation. This applies to any time that you use a translator app or Google Translate to communicate something, whether in person or in writing. And if you are really unsure, try multiple sources.

Hannah T. had an app that had a search function, as well as a scanner to scan and translate text. . . definitely helpful! Again, this is limited by how good the translation is, but in a pinch, it can often get the message across to both students and parents, especially when it is something positive or in person. She often used it when trying to teach one-on-one reading lessons to a non-English speaking student that she had in her class for a time. . . teaching vocabulary words, especially simple nouns and verbs, is the perfect use of basic translation tools!

It is important to develop a great relationship with parents who you may struggle to communicate with throughout the year. Making sure that they know you are all on the same team, that you love and support their child, and that you want to be able to be an effective teacher to their child are so helpful when the inevitable translation faux pas occurs. They will be more willing to hear you out and give you the benefit of the doubt if you have proven yourself trustworthy and caring in the past. Sending home emails in English and another language can be a double-edged sword if you don't have reliable translation services, but hopefully, it will show parents that you are trying to bridge the gap and keep them in the loop as much as possible. Seek the advice of other teachers in your school and on your team to ask them what they do to effectively and regularly communicate with non-English speaking parents.

Sending Things Home

Finding ways to communicate positive, negative, and neutral things in universal ways, such as sticker charts or 'smiley/frowny face' papers for students with behavior plans, is a great way to communicate with parents without using language. Tip from Hannah T.: the parent needs to already be expecting to see a daily paper or sticker because no student will voluntarily give their parent a paper with a frowny face circled.

Having pre-made notes in your desk all printed and cut out makes it much easier to send things home to parents without taking time out of teaching or potentially forgetting to write a note. Especially if they are uniform notes for different things like 'Great problem solving, _____!' or 'I want to be a friend like _____!': parents can know what those are from the beginning of the school year and look forward to their student getting these affirmations. Sending home flyers and newsletters that follow the same format every time and include lots of simple language and visuals helps parents to be in the loop on what is happening in your classroom. Another system to have in place to start the year well!

In-The-Moment Communication

Knowing who in your building is able to translate (and how to contact them) is also important. Some schools have policies about someone who is 'certified' in some way being the only approved method to translate content, while others say to use any ability you may have to try to communicate with parents in their language. When communicating something negative to parents, especially over the phone or in writing, it is much more important that translations be accurate and true to the spirit of what you are trying to say. Think of how in the English language, we might say that a student 'had a hard time' with something instead of 'didn't' do something. We avoid certain words because we know words paint pictures that we may or may not want to paint. When moving across the language barrier, it is important to keep this in mind.

For those who don't have to work through a language barrier, make sure that you are totally ready for the phone call before you sit down to dial the number. Take notes on things you want to be sure to mention, positive, neutral, or negative. Think about how you'll frame things, and maybe even practice a little script. Hannah T.'s heart was always pounding whenever she needed to call parents for any reason, so she always took some deep breaths and focused on staying calm and thoughtful while she was talking. Better to take longer to respond and think through a response than to say something you regret later! In-the-moment communication doesn't need to be scary, and with practice, it will quickly become second nature.

Make Magic Happen:

What's a good way to practice parent communication? With positive things! It's always going to be easier to talk to a parent or send a note home when it's a positive thing! Establishing communication with parents is important, but it's also helpful to find your groove when it comes to parent communication. Have a plan before you call with what you want to say to the parents and caregivers. It will help you stay on track and on point. Also, be sure to document your communication by writing down the date/time that you called and what was discussed. Practice often, and everyone will be happy with all the positive things!

Unstoppable Personal Life

Hearing Bad News While at School

Hannah S. shares a heartwarming story about how her students comforted her on her hardest day of teaching. Growing up, Hannah was privileged to spend many summer nights playing cards and fishing with her late great-grandfather and her great-grams. Not many adults remember their great-grandparents, let alone have two great-grandmas live to their late 90s who could still carry on conversations and reminisce about old times. Her great-grandparents were a major part of her life for 24 years. She shares,

> On a dreary day in January, I awoke to a phone call about one great-grandmother's death. I was surprised because the other grandmother was the one not doing so well at the time. I knew there was nothing I could do at the moment, and I wanted to stick to normalcy, so I got dressed and headed to school. Within minutes of arriving, the secretary walked down to my room and told me to call my mom. In less than two hours, I lost two major role models and dear great-grandmothers. Even though I knew this day was coming, as they were 97 and 99 years old, I was devastated.
>
> That day was a very hard but very humbling day. After crying with my colleagues, I put on a brave face because I wanted to be present for my kids. I'm sure they all picked up on the fact that their teacher wasn't as bubbly as usual and wondered why other adults were coming in to offer condolences to their teacher. The lesson that day was a flop (I actually redid part of it later on), and my heart really wasn't in the day. However, I'll never

forget how kind my kids were to me that day. My students turned a paper in, and, like they often did, they drew me pictures on the back. However, this particular day, the pictures were all so dear and really picked my spirits up.

I never announced why I wasn't as bubbly, but my kids picked up on their teacher's emotions. My kids wrote me the kindest notes and were the sweetest. They truly lifted my spirits and made me think of how simple life is. I still have some of their notes and will always remember the comfort I found that day in my kids."

Hannah's story reminds us of how the little actions of our students can be of great comfort. You are a teacher, but you are also human and will have days where things in your personal life aren't easy. It can be hard to not let those things carry-over into the workplace, but when they do, find comfort in the simple words and actions of your students.

Health Issues

Hannah T. shares, "I started my year off with very scary health issues leading to taking off the entire second week of school for surgery." Yes, she said the second week of school as a first-year teacher! Hannah T. goes on to share, "Less than a month after that, I found myself unexpectedly pregnant with a high-risk pregnancy and extreme sickness called Hyperemesis Gravidarum ('the royal affliction,' as a friend puts it)." She was a newly married, first-year teacher, living in her in-laws' basement, unexpectedly pregnant and the breadwinner. . . it doesn't get much more rock bottom than that. Through all of that, Hannah T. was struggling to keep students moving forward and growing, especially in reading, which led to her being on an improvement plan to be able to keep her job. . . no pressure, right? This is not what she dreamed of when she crossed the stage at graduation.

Hannah T. wasn't sure how she could keep moving forward. And yet, she did. She shares,

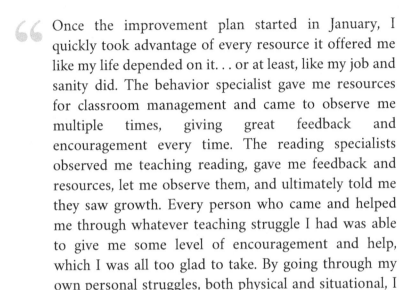 Once the improvement plan started in January, I quickly took advantage of every resource it offered me like my life depended on it. . . or at least, like my job and sanity did. The behavior specialist gave me resources for classroom management and came to observe me multiple times, giving great feedback and encouragement every time. The reading specialists observed me teaching reading, gave me feedback and resources, let me observe them, and ultimately told me they saw growth. Every person who came and helped me through whatever teaching struggle I had was able to give me some level of encouragement and help, which I was all too glad to take. By going through my own personal struggles, both physical and situational, I definitely learned that I could NOT do it on my own.

If I had not tried, my students would have continued to lag and not make gains month after month. Instead, I went from having one 'on grade level' reader at the beginning of the year to having at least eight 'on grade level' at the end of the year. Was that all of my students? Not even close. But every single one of my students made gains throughout the year, both academic and personal, and that is something that I can be proud of.

My daughter was born on the last day of school, so I wasn't able to give my students the goodbye I envisioned, telling each one of them how proud I was of how hard they worked and how much they had helped me learn and grow. Despite the odds, we all made it to the end of the school year, and we had so much to show for it."

While you may not find yourself with health scares or pregnancy to deal with, our biggest piece of advice from Hannah T.'s story is to GET HELP. You can't do it on your own, and you do your students a disservice if you try. Being the best teacher you can be doesn't come without help; you are not alone—nor should you be. There are so many people out there willing to help you. Take advantage of it! Use their help. After all, we are all better together.

Friends, we shared many personal events in this section, and just like us, you will make it through this and come out stronger, better, and wiser because of it. You ARE unstoppable.

4

M: Making It Work

WE'VE DONE some thoughtful reflection on some hard truths of teaching. There is a lot to think about leading up to and throughout that first year: expectations, planning, routines, management, and having a life outside of school. Time to think about all those components of teaching and how they come together. We will do a crash course on making it all work: from classroom management to your own sanity. So, refill your cup, grab those pens, and get comfy!

Making it Work in the Classroom

Classroom management is multifaceted. From managing behaviors to the mundane routines, there is a lot to consider. The first thing to realize, though, is the difference between classroom management and behavior management.

Classroom vs. Behavior Management	The Key to Effective Classroom Management

Classroom management is how you plan to manage your classroom. Simple right? Well, let's think through it more. This involves so much proactive work, from your rules for sharpening pencils to what your system for giving tests will be. A lot of this can be thought through before a single student walks through the door, although it may need a little (or a lot of) tweaking as the school year goes on. There is SO much to think about when it comes to classroom management, and a lot of things you may not even think about until a situation comes up. What is the protocol for throwing away trash? What if a student needs craft materials? Are you going to have a single student pass out all materials, or one from each group come and get it? What materials can students have at their seats? How will they be stored and accessed? For every 1 plan you make, there are 5 situations you probably haven't thought of. But it is <u>way</u> better to go into your school year with 10 planned routines than 0. So, when it comes to classroom management, being proactive is everything! What sort of situations can you think of in advance to prepare for?

Situation	System
❏ Throwing away trash ❏ Entering/Leaving the classroom ❏ Bathroom breaks / Water fountain	❏ ❏ ❏ ❏

Yes, there is a lot to think about. But, as we stated, it is important to be proactive and consider these routines prior to having a classroom of students before you. When proactivity is not applied, classroom management can be a struggle. Hannah T. shares her struggle with classroom management:

 Classroom management was definitely my downfall. I didn't take the time to think through different systems and come into the school year with intention. I thought to myself, *I have ClassDojo. . . the rest will fall into place."*

It wasn't long before her classroom descended into chaos. Hannah needed to be more thoughtful in what the points meant to the class as a whole, what they did to earn points, etc. As a new teacher, you are not going to be prepared to handle every question/situation (some routine and some not so routine) thrown at you. By not being prepared, this may lead to many on-the-spot decisions about how to handle situations, which then could lead to a lot of inconsistency, which, of course, is the biggest no-no in classroom management. Don't be thinking in December, "If only in September I had just had consistent rules, clear expectations, and known consequences, then there would be no discussion of fairness or appeal for mercy."

Consistent **R**ules, clear **E**xpectations, and known **C**onsequences are what we are going to call **REC**. Currently, what's coming to mind is

(W)rec(k) its Ralph (Spencer, 2012)! Maybe you have Ralph in your class, and he hasn't matured his character and actions yet. Friend, you just have to 'REC it' by providing your learners with consistent rules, clear expectations, and known consequences from the beginning. One would think that it is common sense to be proactive and set the stage on the first day of school. However, we did say that teaching is a live & learn experience, and as a new teacher, it is easy to assume these rules, expectations, and consequences are known without you setting the stage. Even if the stage is set, it is easy to turn to survival mode and become inconsistent with consequences or with giving warnings and letting things go.

Make Magic Happen:

Take time to actively think and plan things through. What rules, expectations, and consequences are already put into play by the district? What can you add? How can students get involved in the process? Will you make a class constitution or contract? Will students help determine the REC of your classroom? How will you manage the REC in your classroom? Go back and review your resources in Teacher Expectation 1.

Rules	Expectations	Consequences

Behavior management is a little trickier. You can start to think about it before students come, but it will be dependent on individuals. Every single year, you have a new group of students with new learning needs and new personalities. Maybe every class period provides new challenges as you have a new set of learners every hour. You have to find what works for you and your students. Others may have ideas, or you may get inspiration from talking to fellow teachers, a behavior specialist, or the school counselor, but ultimately, you know your students (and yourself) best to find a way that works.

Friends, you have your own expectations for your classroom management (think back to Teacher Expectation 1). As previously discussed, these expectations for Pinterest worthy management may not hold true... that is, until you get your feet wet and gain some tried and true experience. You may go in thinking you are going to be the understanding teacher, and then realize that some students need a hard line and firm boundaries. You may be able to think about some of the potential behaviors in advance, but you can't really know how you will react when Ben point blank *refuses* to come sit on his spot on the carpet while 18 other kids are sitting there watching you and waiting for your reaction. What will you do in the moment (ITM)? Sure, there are lots of things you can do later, but how will you handle any potential power struggles, disrespect, or defiance ITM? It will take time, practice, experience, and lots of mistakes to find a solution that works for different students in different situations. You may not even find a perfect solution until June... just in time to send Benny to the next teacher and for you to get a whole new classroom of personalities. Just remember: **The only person you can control is yourself.**

Here are some of our general tips when it comes to behavior management!

- Be Intentional: Go into the year with a well thought out plan, stick to that plan, and adjust the plan as needed.
- Be Proactive: Take the time to decide what routines you want for every little thing (sharpening pencil, getting a tissue, throwing things away, bathroom sign-out, paper collection) so you're not caught off guard by a student abusing a privilege.
- Be Consistent: The golden rule. Of course, there is room to admit when you've implemented something that isn't

working, but waffling in every situation and at every turn isn't good for anyone. If you're being intentional and proactive, being consistent will be MUCH easier.

- Be Patient: With yourself and with your students. You've all just met, and it will take time to find what works for all of you in the little community of your classroom.

Make Magic Happen:

Think about how you respond to different situations, and how you prefer to be treated in those situations. Do you like to talk it out, or be given time to think? Are you a people pleaser, or contradictory? If someone calls you out publicly, are you humiliated or grateful? Do you dig in when someone corrects you? These are all potential ways your students could respond in different situations. Take time to know yourself as well as you can, since YOU are the only part of an interaction that you can control.

Making it Work with TIME

You are going to be a busy bee during those first years. By now, you already know that, but one skill you must learn is time management. It goes hand in hand with self-care as a teacher. There is a large turnover with teachers because they burn themselves out. It is so easy to do. Carefully consider the following tips so that you can avoid the "burn out" feeling. Shayla S. says:

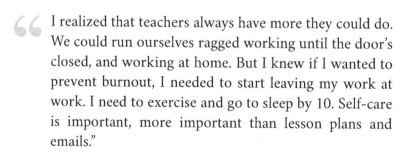

I realized that teachers always have more they could do. We could run ourselves ragged working until the door's closed, and working at home. But I knew if I wanted to prevent burnout, I needed to start leaving my work at work. I need to exercise and go to sleep by 10. Self-care is important, more important than lesson plans and emails."

Maddie B. also shares her story of finding a balance with time management:

 I had to embrace this balance as fluid. There are some weeks where I stay 3 days until 5:30 and 2 days until 9:00. There are other weeks where I leave with the students every single day. The most static factor is REST! I used to believe that it was okay to work all the time because I loved it. In reality, I was burning myself out. I cannot be my best self when I am tired and uninspired, and my students deserve the best."

And it's true! If you aren't taking care of yourself, you aren't able to give your students the best version of you. Not that it will come easily, or quickly. . . in fact as we write these tips and techniques, we are still working on them in our practice too! So, friends, you are not alone.

Time Management Tip 1: Plan ahead when you can!

There are so many ways that you can plan ahead for your teaching day. Maybe during those first few weeks you can come early and stay late, but set a 'leave' time and/or an 'arrive' time for yourself. Don't make it a practice to get home at 9:00 PM regularly. Hannah T. shares, "I learned for myself that I needed to leave school at school, and I needed to leave by 5:30 PM every day." Friends, please try to leave work at work. It can actually help you to be more productive. It can lead you to prioritize the things that you need to do and stay laser-focused every afternoon when the kids leave so that you can get everything done before you need to leave.

Other teachers have a 'take home what I can get done at home' policy that had them out the door by 4:00. Maybe that is something you can do as well, and be able to efficiently grade, plan, and prep from the comfort of your own couch and in your PJs. Who doesn't love to grade in their Snuggy? Or maybe you bounce out of bed early in the morning, get your work done in the morning before the students arrive at school, and you are out the door at dismissal. Whichever speaks to you, figure it out now, don't wait until April for this light bulb to go off. Katy G. shares, "The best advice my mentor gave me was it will eventually get done... maybe not today, but eventually." This is so true; don't set out to get a to-do list of 20 things done today. Instead, pick and choose and try to pare it down to 5.

Time Management Tip 2: Find a healthy balance of work and personal life.

Balance? What is that? We like to think of these more as areas of focus instead of balance. Dr. Sam shares,

> When I have a huge to-do list, I focus on 2 or 3 things I want to get done that day. I like to use the Panera bread strategy of Pick 2! Some days I focus on lectures and activities for the future teachers that I work with; other days, I am recording podcast episodes; other days, I may have a specific blog post I am working on. It works for me, find what works for you!"

Having specific goals for a day, a prep period, or an hour after school can help you laser-focus on what you're doing and be able to have a clear stopping point when you are done.

You *need* to have a life outside of school. Yes, friends—you do. Whether it's roommates, spouses, kids, or friends, you have a life outside of school and people who want to hang out with you. It is important to make time for those relationships and those people around you who lift you up, encourage you, challenge you, and support you. Make time for them on your calendar. Friends, we also encourage you to build relationships with those in your building. Hang out with colleagues outside of the classroom as a way to relax. Learn to just put your work down because you will always have a load of work. Go out and have fun with your colleagues. You never know where a conversation can lead.

Time Management Tip 3: When to say "yes."

During your first couple of years, you will try to be a superhero and get it all done! Be mindful of when to say "yes" to opportunities: both professionally and personally. Say "yes" when you know you will be fulfilled, AND it won't take away from the things that you value, whether that be time with family/friends, hobbies, etc. Don't over commit yourself, but find that perfect balance. Say "yes" to time with your family and friends. Go hiking, go to the beach, take a weekend off of doing any planning for school what-so-ever. Say "yes" to opportunities at school that won't take away from the important things in your life. Better yet, find ways to incorporate the important things in your life at school! Coach a sport that you love, get involved in an after-school program you are passionate about, go to a conference you can share at. Bringing more of you into what you do makes things more enjoyable for everyone!

During her twelve months of learning for her M.S.Ed, Hannah S. found that managing her time was difficult. Hannah recalls that "30 credits while teaching, coaching a spring sport, and keeping family first was a lot at times, but was doable with intentional time management." She offers some advice to teachers of all years: decide what are "musts" and what are "can-do-withouts." Hannah knew that her family came first, and she did not want to miss out on family time because of grading or planning. Sometimes saying 'yes' means saying it to things that are not school-related. Identifying your priorities and saying yes to the ones at the top of the list are important parts of keeping things in balance and being able to fill yourself up.

Time Management Tip 4: How to say "no."

As a teacher, especially a new one, it is so easy to say "yes" to everything, particularly when it comes to serving our schools and classrooms. Here is a secret—it is OK to say "no." We are giving you
permission to do so. Give yourself permission to say NO. Once you
know what you can't do without, you will need to decide what you
can let go of. Make a list with all of the areas of your teaching life—
professional responsibilities, volunteer work, committees, etc.

Are there any areas that are not igniting your passion or that you can
reasonably let go of? If you need to, channel your inner Elsa and "Let
it Go!" (Del Vecho, 2013). Katy G. shares, "During my first year
teaching I volunteered to be the Assistant Coach for Dance Team. . .
even though I have never done dance in my life." Don't say yes to
everything. Instead, find areas of strengths that you have and see if
there is a need for it at the school. If you can't find an area, maybe try
to fill an area with your unique gifts and talents.

For some of us, maybe it isn't about the extras that we do at school, maybe it's the extras we put on ourselves. For example, it might mean giving up the attempt for a perfect activity or Instagram worthy classroom organization. Hannah S. shares, "I spent countless hours scouring for the perfect activity when I already had one that fit the needs of my learners." Now that she has gotten her feet wet, she is spending the time going back and changing out some activities for improvement. However, she is doing it a little at a time. It doesn't all have to be perfect, nor does it have to be done all at once! Friends, don't make sweeping declarations and rework your unit on fractions the night before you introduce it to your students because you found one on Teachers Pay Teachers that is more visually appealing. Instead, make small changes you will eventually rework into a unit, doing it with baby steps and not giant leaps.

Make Magic Happen:

Check out the hashtag #timemanagement on Twitter and Instagram, and also search "Time Management Tips" on Pinterest. Write down what you want to try out this year. Use what works for you, but make sure you pick something that keeps you accountable.

Making It Work for YOURSELF

Friends, set strict boundaries for yourself before the school year starts, and stick to it. For example, maybe you set up a rule that you will not check email after 5:00 PM Monday through Friday, or you have a date night with friends or a loved one every Thursday night. Remember, you are NOT failing your students by helping yourself first. You need to take time for yourself, don't feel guilty about it. You have to invest in yourself to pour into others.

It is like when you are about to take off on a flight: The flight attendant will share with the passengers in the case of an emergency, put your own air mask on first before helping others. As teachers, we cannot help our students if we cannot help ourselves first. Self-care looks different for everyone, but make sure that you are securing your own oxygen before you set out to help others. A bubble bath, a new show, a fancy dinner, or a night out with friends. . . whatever it is that you need to feel rested and refreshed. Take some time to write down ideas for things that you consider self-care.

Keeping yourself healthy and in a positive state of mind is one of the most important things you can do for yourself as an educator. It will be tempting, but don't compare yourself to teachers on Instagram and Pinterest who have the "most creative" ideas and "best organization." Most likely, they have spent years becoming who they are! Some even have given up being in the classroom to create amazing curriculum and themed units. Be you. Stay true to yourself and don't *change* yourself to become another teacher. Learn from others, use their ideas, but don't change who you are.

Surround yourself with positive vibes, especially when you are not feeling so positive yourself. A Pinterest board of inspiring quotes, a list of 'wins' that you've accomplished, notes from students. . . those are all great reminders that you are a teacher of impact and that you have grown to be better. Always remind yourself that everyone is on a journey in their teaching, although they may be at different points. No one, not even the most inspiring Insta account, has 'arrived.'

Personal growth is important to become #eduawesome teachers. As mentioned in the next chapter, using social media is one outlet for professional growth. Another is learning through continuing education. In a year or two, think about going back for additional education. But we caution you to be mindful of how you go about fulfilling those courses. Consider hybrid programs or online courses that will allow flexibility.

Hannah S. shares that during her second year of teaching, she was able to attend a statewide conference with colleagues and administration from her school district. It proved to be a bonding experience for the team where they could share ideas and engage in professional dialogue. In fact, when it came time for her research for my MSEd program, she decided to focus on personalized learning as a result of the professional learning experiences. She was able to blend her professional learning with the pursuit of her degree. Hannah S. went back for her Master of Education degree during her second year of teaching. There were a lot of programs to consider, but when it came down to it, Hannah decided an online program would mesh well with her schedule.

When going back to school after two years of teaching, Dr. Sam chose to pursue a certification and a master's degree online. At first, she went to get a certification in educational technology in order to go after a job placement that she wanted later that year. But after falling in love with the learning, she was able to roll the certification into a Master of Education in Instructional Technology (which later led to a Ph.D.!). To be honest, it was difficult to go back to school and teach full-time. There were long days, and in some cases, long months, but it was worth it for her in the end. In most cases, her graduate work complimented her teaching in the classroom, and she was able to complete assignments and use them in her classroom later that week or month. She was able to apply what she was learning in her course-work directly into her classroom with her students, and it was a great way to develop as an educator and lifelong learner.

This section might not seem important now because you just finally completed your teaching requirements and got your degree. You walked across the stage and into the classroom, and maybe going back to school is the last thing on your mind. That is totally OK! Try to make a plan soon to get back at it—learn more and grow. Maybe you're not ready to go back to school yet, but you will need to find an outlet to recharge yourself because you will get run down! To be an educator of excellence, you must continue to keep a clear mind and a growth mindset. It's okay to have those days when you feel over-whelmed and worn out. But you need to find positive ways to refuel your love for education and learning. Here are some of our ideas (check for the QR codes in chapter 1!):

- Listen to podcasts on your ride to work, either educational or entertainment. . . you are investing in yourself and friends, and that's cool.
- Attend your local Edcamp.

- Continue your education journey—learning doesn't end when you cross the stage at graduation.
- Attend a webinar on a hot topic in education or read a blog series that is of interest to you. Maybe it's an area in which you struggle or want to get better at understanding. Find a topic that is going to push you as a teacher to be better.
- Pursue professional development through your local education organizations. Most are free and low-cost, and, in some cases, you can get continuing professional development hours participating.

Make Magic Happen:

A great tool for any classroom is your education. Think about some areas of education that light your fire and make you feel passionate about teaching and learning. Dr. Sam found a love for educational technology and how it helps to make the impossible, possible for students diagnosed with disabilities. Hannah S. was excited about literacy and mathematics for young learners. What are the fields within education that get you excited? List them below.

A Not-So-Mirror-Image

As we close out this chapter, always remember that what works for someone else may or may not work for you. Remind yourself of this whenever you are trying something that seems like it's not working. Reflect, re-evaluate, and make changes where you need to. Only YOU know what will work for you in these areas! Make a plan, you got this.

5

A: All in This Together

FOR SOME OF YOU, the theme to *High School Musical* (Schain, 2006) just played through your head. Teaching is no longer a profession where you can close the doors to your classroom, only leaving to go to the bathroom and for lunch duty. Teaching is about building a community within your school, your district, and your community. It is about opening your doors for collaboration with teachers down the hall, across the state, and across the world! Teaching nowadays blows the doors off the hinges, allowing you to invite experts into the classroom and to connect with children and schools around the world.

Connecting Virtually

If you are looking for ideas on Instagram or Twitter, you might have come across the term PLN, which stands for Professional Learning Networks. PLNs are people you choose to follow because you have a common interest, and they can choose to follow you back. In this mutual partnership, you will share ideas, ask questions, and collaborate. These are very powerful groups that you will have to create on your own. However, the benefits are endless, and they take time to grow. These groups are not about the quantity of followers, but the quality. Dr. Sam. talks about how she teaches her students to use their PLNs:

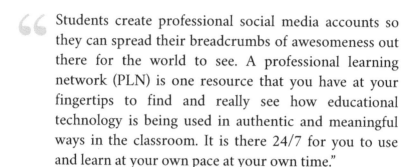

> Students create professional social media accounts so they can spread their breadcrumbs of awesomeness out there for the world to see. A professional learning network (PLN) is one resource that you have at your fingertips to find and really see how educational technology is being used in authentic and meaningful ways in the classroom. It is there 24/7 for you to use and learn at your own pace at your own time."

It really is a resource for you to use at your own pace, on your own time, and in your own way. There is no one 'right' way to use your PLN, but it is essential to have one!

PLNs include those that you physically meet and interact with, but you can cast your net of knowledge so much further when you use social media. By using Twitter or Instagram, you can really own your professional development and look to find resources that are going to speak to you as an educator of excellence, crowdsourcing pro tips from all around the world! Here are a few tips to help you harness your positive professional presence using Twitter and/or Instagram:

- Include a professional bio pic of just YOU.
- In your bio, include your WHY (Why do you teach? Why do you want to impact the lives of students around the world?).
- Be yourself, both personally and professionally. Let people see and connect with both sides of you as you hopefully make lasting friendships with those near and far.
- Be engaged! Whether it be through Twitter chats or regular Insta posts, start conversations through questions, thoughts, and reflection.

Being a connected educator will help you gain insight into new trends, new tools to help students, and new ideas. You might first want to start your journey on Twitter. Create an account, add a photo, include a bio, and go on a following spree. Find a trusted educator and look at the people they follow. . . that's a good place to start. Join a couple of Twitter chats, even just to lurk, and follow people who say things that inspire or grow you. From Twitter, you can move into the real world in the form of Edcamps and other conferences, meeting people in real life that you can connect with virtually after sharing ideas in person. Building a PLN beyond the walls of your classroom and school building is one of the most important things you can do in the modern world of education. . . as George Couros (2016) says, "Isolation is a choice." If you feel alone. . . well, part of that is on you.

Make Magic Happen:

Check out some thoughts veteran teachers had to share!

#NT2t chat, September 14, 2019: Tips and Tricks for New Teachers

Katy G. goes beyond the walls of the classroom when collaborating. In today's world, everyone is collaborating globally, and it is important to teach our students to have a global mindset. If you are teaching middle school or younger, these will be important skills for your students to have going into their future careers. It also helps them have a more open mind to new cultures and backgrounds that they may have never been introduced to before. There are some wonderful programs that are available or that a teacher can choose to set up themselves.

For those teachers that want to make a very memorable experience for their students and connect with their curriculum, here is a story of Katy G.'s experience while she was still a pre-service teacher:

> I wanted to make the book *Number the Stars* by Lois Lowry really come to life for my students. It was historical fiction, so it had a lot of potential opportunities. I started small and contacted the Holocaust Center of Pittsburgh. Unfortunately, they were unable to find a time that would fit with the students' schedule, so I went a little bigger and contacted the United States Holocaust Memorial Museum. They had more opportunities that I was excited about, but unfortunately, again, it came down to the time frame. I wanted this moment for the students to be impactful, especially hearing it from the individuals who experienced it themselves because the unfortunate reality is most of these survivors will not be around much longer to share their stories in person.
>
> After the last two roadblocks, I decided to take a long shot at contacting The Danish Jewish Museum in Copenhagen, Denmark. If you are familiar with the novel, the setting of the story is in Denmark during World War II when Denmark was occupied by the Germans. I didn't think I would get in contact with anyone at the center, but I knew the worst thing that could happen is they would tell me no or ignore my email. Despite my doubts, I received an email telling me they would arrange to have a survivor discuss her experiences as a child during World War II. The survivor that was chosen to speak had a very similar story to the girls in the novel: She had to be smuggled out of Denmark and lived in Switzerland for a time. This woman's story was parallel to the fictional

characters in the story. Not only was I able to set up a Skype interview for the class I was teaching, but I was able to set up a second one for an entire grade level to listen to.

I was ecstatic for the students. These types of opportunities are slowly dwindling, and there will eventually not be first-person accounts that can happen live. The future children will only know the stories through recorded interviews and written documents."

Katy really created an incredible opportunity for her students using resources that were available to her on an international level. If you are still trying to get outside resources, but don't have the time to explore opportunities, here are a few other resources to check out:

- For science teachers, there is a wonderful program called *Skype a Scientist*. Teachers can go on the website and fill out a Google Form (for each class you need a scientist). You can select which type of scientist you want to talk to your students. The program will reach out to you when they have a scientist that aligns with your timeframe. This program is a fantastic opportunity for students to explore professions they may never have known about prior. Especially in rural communities where professionals that students interact with are very limited at times. Therefore, these events need to be scheduled to spark the students' interest.
- *Skype in the Classroom* is another way to bring in virtual field trips, guest speakers, classroom to classroom interactions, and more. There are even opportunities with celebrities. Jane Goodall was a special guest for one month, but you have to keep an eye on these opportunities so you can sign up. There are many different journeys to explore with this organization. It works best for educators to do research before using it. Hannah T. was a guest speaker for a Skype in the Classroom

in Brazil, answering their questions about her culture as opposed to theirs, and helping students realize that they had lots of pop cultural connections in common with people that seemed impossibly far away.

- *Mystery Skype* is a great way to connect your students with students around the world, helping them to learn about other cultures and what life is like for kids just like them who live life very differently. Especially after learning about other cultures or countries, students could connect with a class in that place and have concrete learning to put with their abstract learning.

Skype A Scientist	Skype in the Classroom	Mystery Skype

Building Collaboration

Our students come to school with so many needs and goals. It is up to us to work with our colleagues towards the main goal of educating students the best that we can, keeping students at the forefront. Collaboration is key to provide the best student-centered education. This can happen through partnerships, co-teachers, administration, and families.

Partnerships can come in many forms, in and out of the classroom. Partnerships with your colleagues, peers, administration, parents, and classroom helpers can all make your classroom a place for students to feel welcomed and valued. Partnerships with your colleagues are some of the most valuable relationships because they are the people who also know your students, their stories, and their needs. Hannah S. shares, "My team and I have a connection that is unique and special. We are constantly sharing ideas, helping each other, and are just there for each other. Over the years, my colleagues have become like family, and I am very grateful for that!"

Relationships with your coworkers are essential! Building a professional relationship with your colleagues as a first-year teacher can be a little daunting. You don't have to be teacher besties with your colleagues, or even family-like, but you do have to work professionally together. Students can sense when there is something amiss, or relationships are strained. We recommend connecting with colleagues by building a relationship at the personal level. Connect in areas outside of teaching that you can share with your colleagues.

Make Magic Happen:

It can sometimes feel like you are trying to force friendships, and it shouldn't be that way. Even being able to have casual conversations with coworkers can be a huge step in building relationships with them. Maybe you are a hockey fan, and you notice that your colleague has a sign for the local hockey team on their bulletin board—strike up a conversation. Some other ways to get the ball rolling include:

- Listen and have conversations with your grade level partners.
- Make a note of when their birthday is and put a card in their mailbox.
- Ask them about their weekends and family.
- Don't be afraid to ask questions—as situations arise, write them on a sticky note so you can ask a colleague about it later in the day.
- Don't be afraid to answer questions and speak up. Just because you don't have tenure or three years of teaching experience doesn't mean you don't have ideas and value to share.
- Share your ideas when questions arise in team meetings. You

don't need to agree with everything your colleague has to say, and that's fine. That's how we reflect and grow as educators. However, don't ever argue with another individual when you disagree. That's just unprofessional and causes unnecessary tension.

- Share your ideas and big wins, but also share what you are struggling with in the classroom.
- Make time to talk to your colleagues before or after school in team meetings.

Co-teachers

When it comes to co-teaching, first things first: we need to stop calling students "their students" and "my students." All students in the class are "our students." Don't you want all students to succeed in your class? Therefore, in a co-teaching situation, all students are both teachers' students. We like to refer to co-teaching as two certified educators working together to help all students succeed. Try to keep that definition in mind as we continue our discussion about co-teaching.

Each co-teaching experience will be different because we all have our own personalities, and there are also different methods of co-teaching. Meet with your co-teacher, bounce ideas, use each other's skills in the classroom. How will you go about working together? What form of co-teaching will you be using? Will you be flexible with this? Find a common time to plan to get on the same page- sometimes having virtual meetings for shared lesson plans can really save time for busy teachers. If your school uses something like Planbook to write and share lesson plans, sharing Planbooks with your co-teacher is certainly an invaluable resource! Not only will it help you both be better coordinated and able to flow together with your content, but it allows you to see how someone else writes lesson plans, what they include, and how they plan ahead of time to make units cohesive. Definitely something that can be challenging as a teacher! Co-teaching is a shared experience, so share in the planning as in the teaching.

You are especially lucky if your co-teacher is someone with years of experience, like Hannah T.! She had an ESOL teacher who pushed into her room in the morning; she learned SO much from watching her work and asking her questions. It helped that nearly all her students worked with this amazing ESOL teacher, and so she could incorporate into her own lessons what the other teacher had worked on with them. She also saw it as a learning opportunity for her. . . she watched here and there while she worked with reading groups across the room, and asked the other teacher during planning periods what she was doing at certain points or how she went about teaching certain concepts. It was through and because of that co-teacher that she learned how to teach writing to students by building upon past skills and building up throughout a unit, helping students to go from "I do" to "We do" to "You do." It is so empowering as a teacher to see your students grow in such concrete ways!

What happens if co-teaching is not going as planned? Refer back to our suggestions and thoughts in the Teacher Expectations 2 section of Chapter E. We are all in this together for our students. That means two teachers are working cohesively in the co-teaching environment. There are many great resources out there to help both teachers get on the same page and plan for a phenomenal co-teaching experience.

Co-Teaching: How to Make it Work
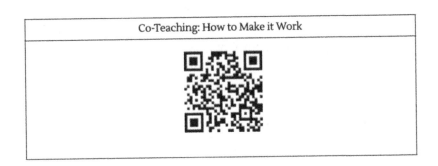

Administration

While sometimes you may not have a positive relationship with admin, or may be unsure what your relationship with them is, at least you can know that they are working for the same goal you are. Sometimes there is a bigger picture that we can't see, and they need to be thinking about the long game. In the same way you are responsible for the learning of a whole class, they are responsible for the learning of a whole school, plus the growth and development of their faculty. With a lot on their plate, it can sometimes seem like they are being tough on you, but really, they are trying to push you to help your students the way they need to be helped. They know the community of a school and the needs of most students in a school family. They are a great resource to help you understand the 'vibe' of a school and the needs of the students in the community. You are always on the same team, with the same goals in mind. . . helping students succeed. Hannah T. shares her story:

 When I was first told that I was underperforming in November, I was so discouraged and felt like I didn't even know where to begin to fix myself. The way an improvement plan worked in my district was that you had a month of, essentially, probation, and if you weren't able to show adequate growth during that period, then you went on a formal improvement plan. I, of course, wasn't able to make adequate growth in one month and so I was put on a formal improvement plan just before going into winter break. I remember meeting with my principal and assistant principal to figure out the domain I was looking to improve in, the goals for my students, and what all the improvement plan would entail when we came back after winter break. Up until that point, I had been very quiet in all of our meetings out of a combination of emotional pregnancy hormones and not being sure what to say. I finally ended the meeting by telling her that I was *glad* to be on an improvement plan and that I wanted to improve myself so that I could be better for my students. I didn't view it as disciplinary, but as a much-needed opportunity for growth for the sake of my students. I hope that I was able to convey it well since I said it through tears despite meaning every word and feeling stronger after I was done. Learning to view my failures as opportunities to grow was such an important step for me to stop feeling defeated."

You may not be the super rockstar teacher you imagined you were going to be—YET. We teach our students to have a growth mindset, and we need to foster that as well! You may have colleagues, parents, or people at weekly improvement plan meetings telling you that you are failing or not growing. But you have control of your growth over time, whether it takes a month, three months, the whole school year, or a new school! When you can see growth in yourself and your students, despite what others may be telling you, then all the struggles and failures are worth it. The end of Hannah's story is that week after week she obtained 'no progress' to 'little progress' on her improvement plan, but the encouraging words she heard from those who observed and mentored her, and the improvements she saw in her students both academically and personally, showed her that she was growing along with her students.

It can be intimidating to have people in and out of your classroom observing, co-teaching, and working with students. But, don't worry, it won't take long to feel comfortable with other professionals coming in and out of the classroom, and you will realize that their observations and feedback are an important part of growing your teaching!

Make Magic Happen:

Friends, it is so important to ask for help. Ask for help from your administration, co-workers, and your PLN. Please don't be afraid to speak up and ask. You never know what can happen as a result of a conversation. View your administration as mentors, whether they do that through 'tough love' or compassion.

Families

As those who are familiar with Charlotte Danielson (2007) know, collaboration with families is essential for building a bridge between home and school. Determine who comprises the "family" of your students and then connect with them on a personal level, not just through weekly newsletters and phone calls about poor choices. Send home shout-outs for the little things. Maybe a student is struggling with behaviors but was a great helper during class. Or, maybe a student who does not normally volunteer offered his or her ideas to the class. Celebrate the wins, the little things, the positives. Be intentional and connect. Look back in Chapter U under 'Unbreakable Communication' to get some ideas. Making a point to send small, regular notes home can help your relationships with students and families in a huge way; students look forward to getting those sorts of pictures or notes to take home and proudly show off!

Don't just give feedback, ask for it from parents. Have parents complete surveys about their child to gain information about strengths and weaknesses, hobbies, home life. Check in throughout the year and ask how things are going. Often parents and guardians can provide insight into school feelings, homework situations, or studying habits that we are unable to be pinpointed at school. Be a team and work with families to provide the best education for each child.

Make Magic Happen:

Connecting with parents and families is vital. Maybe you can contact five families a week. Or, maybe you can send home notes. How are you closing the gap between home and school? What can you do to improve home-school communication? Brainstorm some ideas or goals:

We may all be in this together as educators, but sometimes it doesn't feel that way. Maybe you are in a school environment where you don't feel supported or seen, and there isn't anyone you've 'clicked' with to get through it. It may be the case that the school you are in isn't a good fit for you. . . and that is okay! Maybe you thought your passion was reaching low income or underperforming students, but in reality, you just don't have the experience, support, or skill set to make the biggest impact. That's okay! You are still growing. If a school environment is not encouraging or growing you, move on from there and see it as a huge learning experience for you. Let it inform you of what you are looking for in a district, school, and team. Hopefully, you will be able to find a new school that is a better fit, knowing what sort of things to be looking for and asking about during interviews and observations.

While finding a job may seem like the most important thing coming out of college, finding the *right* job will ensure that you have many more years in a fulfilling career. So, don't give up! Reflect on your year and your environment, seek encouragement and support from those outside of your four walls, and move on to a place where you can be the most effective.

If we can remember that we are all working toward the same goal, it will help us overcome differing personalities and methods to find a solution or compromise that will help our students succeed. So get out there and collaborate. . . for our kids!

6

G: Getting Ready

ONE OF THE biggest ideas new teachers look forward to completing is.
. . drum roll please. . . setting up your OWN classroom! You finally
have that set of keys and space to make your own. You have so many
grand ideas and visions for what your space will look like. Take a
moment to draw, jot down, mind map those ideas.

You're excited to jump in and get things done! There is a LOT to think through as you go about setting up a classroom, not just in terms of where things will go or what your theme may be, but also what your routines and procedures will look like. Keep in mind these helpful tips and tricks as you begin that new year set up and prep. To help you get started, we put together checklists to help you think through the essentials of a classroom set up- you're welcome! Work through this chapter section by section as you think about what your classroom will look like, how it will feel, and how it will run.

Classroom Layout and Organization

This is probably the thing you've most dreamed about, thanks to Pinterest! How your classroom is set up is important to make sure that things flow smoothly and that you actually enjoy being in your room. Especially if you are going to be there early or stay late, you need to make sure that your room 'sparks joy' for you, in the words of Marie Kondo (Kondo & Hirano, 2014). Your classroom layout needs to strike that delicate balance between practical and aesthetical. Below are some things to keep in mind on the practical side of things, but only YOU can answer if your classroom ultimately sparks joy for you and your students.

- Student desk arrangement- how do you want the students' desks to be arranged (rows, small groups, pairs, tables, etc.)?
- Where do you want your desk? Do you even NEED a desk? Many teachers are going deskless these days. You may want to pursue that design.

Ditching the Desk by Nicholas Provenzano in Edutopia

- Where do you need to keep emergency information (fire drill lists, emergency situations, building layout, etc.)? On the trim of the door? In an emergency backpack?
- Do you have easy access to teacher essentials (grades, flexible groups, seating charts, etc.)?
- How many bulletin boards do you have?
- What information needs to be posted all year?
- What information will you switch out as the year/unit's progress?
- What things need to be organized for your convenience? What things need to be organized for student convenience?
- What kind of atmosphere do you want to portray in the classroom? We like the term *atmosphere* instead of *theme* because an atmosphere is something that can carry you throughout the year, such as *kindness counts, teamwork makes the dream work*, etc.

Classroom Routines and Procedures

This is where you can make or break the year. As we've talked about already, classroom routines and procedures are SO important when it comes to classroom management. . . an ounce of prevention is worth a pound of cure! While there are so many things to think about for possible scenarios that may arise, thinking of your system in advance for as many things as you can, is hugely helpful for the first time a student asks to throw something away or get a tissue. Here are some routines, big and small, that we've thought of to get you started:

- How will the morning routine look? Where is the lunch count, backpacks, notes? Do your students do lunch count in your room? How would you like to manage student late work?
- How are you getting your students' attention during whole group, small group, independent work, etc.? You might want to do different signals for each one. During whole group, you might have the students respond back with a saying or hand clap. For independent work, you could have a countdown, so it does not interrupt the students' concentration.
- What are your routines for *every little thing*? Getting a tissue, throwing away trash, moving from the carpet to the desks/tables, turning out the lights. . . these things are not a problem until they suddenly are, and you are scrambling for an idea you won't regret in 2 months.
- How do you organize your resources? Do you have a filing cabinet (and how will it be organized)? Are your things stored in cubbies? Do you have a desk?

30-Minute File Cabinet Makeover

- What materials are readily available to learners? How do you have these accessible for all learners? What are the procedures for using and getting these materials?
- What tasks can you delegate to students? Will you implement

this system right away? How will you teach it to your students?

- How will you make your expectations clear to students? Is the procedure something you can be consistent in, even in different situations? How will you have students practice the procedure so they can get it right?
- What are procedures that students can help develop? Are there classroom systems or rules that they can help decide?

Technology

Technology is definitely a blessing in the classroom unless you can't get it to work. Making sure you have everything figured out, or have a backup plan, will save you a lot of wasted time with students staring blankly and starting to get fidgety while you figure things out.

- What do you have access to? Make a list here of the technology tools you have in your classroom.

- Do you know how the technology works? Can you operate

the projector/laptop/interactive whiteboard, etc.? These are legitimate questions- if you don't know how something works, look up the company on YouTube or Google and figure it out before the kids get there!

- Can you login to the computer? OK, OK, we know that this one sounds weird, but Dr. Sam couldn't get into her computer when working in K-12 for a week after school started. So, make sure you can get into your computer and that you can access:
- School email
- Grade portal
- Attendance portal
- Any shared folders or documents with your teaching team
- Is there a computer cart that your grade band shares- how and when will you access it? Is there a certain procedure you need to follow to get access to the cart of laptops, iPads, etc.?
- How are you storing your students' data and information? Are you using an excel spreadsheet, word document, or another form? Your administration will be very impressed with you if you can collect your data in an organized way that anyone can understand. Or they may have a standardized way to collect it. . . make sure to find out!
- What is your technology procedure in your classroom? Friends, it is the 21st century; technology is not an event; it is not something you do in a separate class. How will YOU meaningfully integrate technology into your classroom?
- What is your policy for students who don't want to participate in something like GoNoodle? This may seem unthinkable, but Hannah T. experienced it herself and was at a loss throughout the entire year on how to handle it!
- Lastly, what is your failsafe backup plan? This may differ from lesson to lesson or subject to subject depending on what you were going to use the technology for, but it is CRUCIAL to have a backup plan any time you are going to use technology for a key part of a lesson or routine.

Keeping yourself sane

Being organized is important and can go a long way in helping you not lose your mind. Check out *Getting Ready Tip 4* later. There are also other self-care things that you should try to plan for in advance, although you may need to adjust and change things throughout the school year or when certain times are busier than others. But never lose sight of the fact that if you are not performing your best, your students are missing out.

- How do YOU want to start your day? Will you prep for that day at the beginning of it, or before you leave the day before? What do you need to have in place before students walk through the door every day to feel ready?
- What are the sorts of things that stress you out? Clutter? Visual noise? If you are stressed out, nobody is winning, so make sure your view from wherever you may sit or stand isn't going to make you want to pull your hair out.
- If you get overwhelmed in the middle of the lesson, how are you refocusing yourself? There will be some days the students just are not on task, talking over you, or you are worried about some personal situations. Katy G. keeps a picture on her desk that sparks happiness when she looks at it during the school day. When she is feeling stressed and overwhelmed, she looks at it for a moment and takes a breath to reset herself.
- At the beginning of the year (sometimes the week before school starts), there are professional development days that you need to attend. Write them down on a calendar or in your digital calendar as soon as you know about them, so you don't forget them.

Edumagicians, keep these lists handy and add to them as you feel necessary for your particular situation. Any other things that may come to mind? Jot them down now before you overlook them. Improvise, adapt, and overcome.

Your classroom is exactly that: YOURS. What worked for Crafty Caitlin on Pinterest may not work for you. You probably already have those Pinterest boards and Teachers Pay Teachers (TPT) resources for organizational hacks, classroom layouts, and the trendiest themes. But remember, you are just as unique as your learners. Decorate in your own style. Use the hacks that work for you and your space. Design a layout conducive to the learning environment of your kiddos. It's ok to scour the internet and social media for ideas, but ultimately it comes down to you. Stay unique by keeping in mind these helpful tips.

Getting Ready Tip 1: Ask for Help from Others

Yes, you have YOUR space, but sometimes it is hard to know where to begin when that to-do list gets long (as it will at the beginning of the year). You are not the only teacher in the building. Use your neighbors to bounce ideas off, reach out for guidance about questions that may arise, or to simply ask for help. Hannah S. was the queen of asking questions during her first year. Four years later, the teachers are still teasing her about "Question?!" Here are some questions that you may find yourself asking:

- What are the procedures for _____?
- Where can I find _____?
- Who can I talk to about _____?
- Do we have any extra _____?
- Where can I get _____?

Use your colleagues for more than just answers to questions. Get inspired by their work. Wander around during prep week to see what other teachers are doing in their classrooms, ask questions, ask others to come look at your room and give practical feedback. Sometimes it is beneficial to have another set of eyes. Hannah T. liked to wander into other classrooms throughout the year to see what other teachers may have changed to fit the current unit, or to get ideas in areas she was struggling in. Seeing other teacher's setups could also help you troubleshoot problems in your routines and procedures or get some more chaotic moments of the day under control. The idea that the smartest person in the room IS the room also extends to your teaching team. . . the smartest person on the team IS the team! Be sure to take advantage of that as you prepare your classroom.

Getting Ready Tip 2: Change and Improve

Changing up your classroom can be easily done through bulletin boards and door decor. Often times, teachers have a bulletin board in their classroom that changes with the seasons, months, holidays, or theme of the year. We would encourage you to get your students involved in this process of thinking through bulletin board content. One way to do this is by having a board dedicated to showcasing student work. This can change every week or month- divide your board into sections or by how many students are in the class, and they each have their own space to design and display their proud moments in your class. What is great about this idea is that everyone can display something a little different to show their unique talents and skills throughout the year. In middle and high school, you can have students decorate the door for themes or holidays. This gives them something to do during homeroom, and it is a great creative outlet. Plus, it saves you time!

Something that can be harder to change throughout the year can be organizational systems or procedures, but if something isn't working for you or your students, then it has got to go! If you can identify a part of the day, a transition period, or a procedure that always seems to bring questions or confusion from students, then it is something that you need to troubleshoot and fix. Ask around with other teachers (see Tip 1), talk to your PLN, and maybe even consult Pinterest for ideas of how to do better in areas where you and your class may be struggling. Admitting that something isn't perfect is the only way to make it better!

Getting Ready Tip 3: Be Practical, Even When It's Not Pretty

You may get to survival periods. . . more important that students are learning and that you are sane than that things are magazine-ready. Katy G. learned that there is no perfect classroom when she organized and reorganized her desk several times during the first few months of teaching. She struggled because she needed time to figure out how she wanted things to work and where she needed things to be.

The most important benefit that can come out of your classroom set up is that your students learn. Sometimes pretty has to be sacrificed for practical. It is a different kind of beauty to watch students be able to independently get materials and have the confidence to have an active role in your classroom setup and organization. After all, if our classroom is all about building community with our students, shouldn't we be working together to make a classroom environment we all enjoy and understand? Things do need to work for you, but they also need to work for your students of all ages.

Make Magic Happen:

You should walk into your classroom for the first time with some sort of plan, but once you are there, try experimenting! Hannah T. definitely recommends physically moving things around to see how they look, maybe even leaving something set up a certain way for a few hours or days (depending on how much time you have before students come) to see how you like it. Try to think through any possible negatives of a certain setup and how you could navigate or mitigate any problems.

Getting Ready Tip 4: Stay Organized

Katy G. was creative and found organizational hacks on Pinterest that she slowly incorporated. One of her favorite hacks was using a filing cabinet to organize her units by title. This made it easy to see the titles of each unit with materials behind it. Hannah S. highly recommends this tool, as well! See the 30 Minute File Cabinet Makeover in the Classroom Routines and Procedures section of this chapter. One thing is for sure: stay organized as you complete units! Keep materials and centers together in an organized way. Katy started keeping things organized and ordered bins to help with the organization. It was a year-long process to organize as she went, but it was worth it. Katy warns, "Don't compare yourself and change simply to be 'Pinterest-worthy.'" Hannah T. also took about half the year to find an organization system that worked for her to keep all of her materials from past units organized. What finally motivated her to find a long-term solution was when she realized that if she didn't keep it all organized, she would be back at square one when it came to materials the following year or at a future school. . . yikes!

If you don't have a good planner or online calendar, get one. If you aren't a person who uses one, consider becoming a "planner" or finding a means of staying organized. You will get a slew of dates for meetings, professional learning community (PLC) meetings, testing days, due dates, etc. You will also need to make sure that you are prepared for the day (copies are made, materials are out, etc.). The key to keeping all those things straight: stay organized. Some suggestions to help you do that:

Transfer all important dates from the district and school calendar into your personal calendar (color code by category, even)

- Due dates: yearly Student Learning Objectives evaluations, IEP input reports
- Faculty Meetings
- Parent-Teacher Conferences
- Flex/Half Days
- Professional Development Days
- Inservice Days
- Professional Learning Community (PLC) Meetings
- IEP Meetings
- Grades/Report Cards Due
- Field Trips
- Assemblies
- Open House
- Other: _____

Plan/Prepare Units

- Copy in advance to avoid morning fights with the copier
- Have materials ready the night before (in case you oversleep or become ill)
- Keep your sub folder/binder handy in case you are out
- Know a general idea of where you are heading with the content tomorrow (Remember: good teachers adjust for their learners, so be flexible but have a general plan.)
- Keep work together for absent students

Hannah T. learned time and time again the importance of having sub plans always ready (or at least being able to type them up the night before) and knowing where you are going with something. When she was very unexpectedly put on bed rest for a week towards the end of her pregnancy, she felt (slightly) less scrambled to get plans together for a sub since she had her sub plan template, her fallback plans, and a clear understanding of where certain subject units were going. That should always be the goal! If you were to suddenly not be able to go into your classroom one day, maybe even for a whole week, would you have something to send to a sub or team member?

Make Magic Happen:

Being organized and prepared will help your sanity! Edumagicians, we challenge you to get into the habit of having things ready for the next day before leaving school: lesson plan out (in case of an unplanned absence), materials ready, objectives and homework written on the board. Mornings can be unpredictable at times. You may find yourself waking up late or sick, or your child needs to go to the doctor. Regardless of what may come of the few hours or minutes before school, help yourself by staying organized.

Getting Ready Tip 5: Don't Fall Behind

It is so easy to fall further and further behind. Be productive and meaningful with your time. Make a to-do list of things that need to happen and decide on a plan of action for accomplishing those things. Maybe that means going to school thirty minutes early and staying thirty minutes after to get things done. Or, maybe it means that each weekday is dedicated to a specific task (Monday: plan lessons for next week, Tuesday: meet with co-teacher about next week, Wednesday: copy for next week, Thursday: get caught up, Friday: reflect on the week). Hannah S. is not a morning person, so she is not very productive before school. However, she likes to have a general plan for each day, get lessons scheduled by Wednesday, and copies made by Friday. She avoids trying to survive and stay afloat when she is able to plan ahead with a proactive and productive plan. Although Hannah remembers many mornings as a new teacher and teacher in grad school overwhelmingly trying to get the copier to go faster in the morning and trying to survive day to day. . . she highly does not recommend that!

Make Magic Happen:

Don't be like the overwhelmed Hannah. Be prepared Hannah. Have a plan, stick to it, and be proactive and productive with your time. Make a plan for how you can stay ahead.

Getting ready may be one of the most exciting things once you get those keys! Go in with a plan, and you won't regret it one minute! Remember, that plan may be drastically altered. But, changing the plan for the better is a great pay-off!

```
┌─────────────────────────────────┐
│                                 │
│                7                │
│                                 │
│          I: Inspiration         │
│                                 │
└─────────────────────────────────┘
```

FRIENDS, we know that teaching can be hard—no one said it would be easy. It has been a long road to even get to your own classroom, and now it's not exactly a walk in the park either. But keeping your inspiration, your 'why,' in the front of your mind will help you get through the days that feel long. Inspiration is like a fountain; while you are there and you are drinking from it, it seems like you will never be thirsty again! But when you are far away in the desert, it's hard to remember just how that cool, cool water felt, and how refreshing it was for your soul. When you are in the deserts of teaching, on the days that you feel down or discouraged, it is so important to be able to quickly revisit that fountain and refresh yourself so that you can continue on in your journey. Inspiration can come from within and without, and this chapter will explore what it looks like to find inspiration in different (and sometimes unexpected) areas.

Inspiration from Yourself

You have to be able to inspire and encourage yourself. Let's face it. . . you wouldn't even BE in this career if you hadn't been inspired by something that lit a spark in you that led to you continually inspiring yourself during all the ups and downs. Let's start first and foremost with your WHY. On those tough days, those really rough days, it's important—mission-critical—that you remember your WHY. Our WHYS ought to be focused on our students. We all should strive to help our students become better versions of themselves. How can you be the difference-maker for your students? How can you help your students become difference makers? Think about and write it down: "Why are you a teacher?" Write your thoughts in the box below, and then we will share our 'whys' with you!

Dr. Sam

Everyone's why changes from time to time throughout their teaching career. For example, Dr. Sam taught students with special needs for four years, and her WHY was "to help students be as independent as possible." She now teaches future educators in the areas of special education and educational technology. She teaches "to impact students that she will never meet through the work of the future teachers she impacts through college courses, her book: EduMagic a

Guide for Preservice Teachers (Fecich, 2018), and through social media."

Hannah S.

Hannah S. thinks back to her WHY when she was a pre-service educator. For as long as Hannah can remember, she wanted to go to Culinary Arts school and eventually open her own "mom and pop" restaurant in rural America. After a job shadow towards the end of her junior year of high school, Hannah realized that she no longer wanted to have a culinary career and that she liked kids. So, she decided to be a teacher! Her WHY: she liked children. Now, two degrees and some matured ideas later, Hannah's WHY has evolved from simply liking children to her desire to inspire children to be thinkers and do-ers. She teaches because she believes that someone has to have faith in a child and show him or her that they can succeed. She teaches because children matter.

Hannah sees students as individuals, which has allowed her to connect with them in unique and special ways. Connecting with students can be, at times, easier than connecting with families and parents. Don't let that obstacle stop you in your tracks. Exhaust all measures to hurdle those obstacles. Refer back to Chapter U for suggestions about handling these challenges. One tough obstacle is closing the home-to-school gap. How can that gap become smaller? Become the bridge. Hannah S. shares that bridging the gap starts with intentionality. We are all a piece in the puzzle of success. Hannah shares, "Together, we can make a difference in the lives of our children who will grow to be difference makers."

Katy G.

Katy remembers sitting in her first education class, which was education psychology. She had just switched her major to Middle-Level Math and Science from Electrical Engineering. She felt very overwhelmed before the class even started. Her colleagues in the room knew they wanted to be educators since high school, but NOT KATY! She had so much information to catch up on. Her first assignment was to create a metaphor of her teaching philosophy (she first had to figure out what a teacher philosophy meant). She settled on the metaphor of a boat to represent her students, and lighthouse to represent Katy as an educator.

Here is what her metaphor meant before going into her background story of why Katy teaches. She feels as an educator, she needs to provide the materials, resources, and information to her students as best as possible. However, it is up to the students to use these resources to guide them to their goal, which would be the land in her metaphor.

Katy is very motivated to provide her students with the tools and equipment they need to succeed in this fast-changing world. Teaching has changed in this modern age, and the jobs that are available today will be different for her students in the future. Katy also has a rounded perspective of being an advocate for students going to college or trade schools since most of her family is in some type of trade-related job. She wants to teach her students to be life-long learners and show them that learning can be fun! Katy says, "I always wanted to be the teacher that I wished I had growing up. I needed a certain type of teacher, especially in high school, when I sometimes felt lost. I want to be the lighthouse that helps boats get to shore in their own way."

Hannah T.

Hannah developed her 'why' throughout her elementary and special education classes. As she interacted with more and more students, both in the mainstream classroom and the special education classroom, she realized that every student is capable of success. . . by different definitions. She was determined to help each student find *their* definition of success and how they could achieve it. Her 'why' was summed up like this: "I teach to help each student achieve success, by their standards." That doesn't mean that some students don't have to learn to read or do math, but that every student has a goal that they can always be working toward and seeing progress in themselves. When we only set our own goals for students, they are not invested stakeholders; we need them to be to have an active part in their education. Rather, we need to help each student find their strengths and dreams, thus giving them a reason to be invested in the tools you are going to share with them. By seeing how inspired our students are about their progress and education, we will also inspire ourselves to keep teaching them.

Maybe you can relate to one of our whys, or maybe your why is completely different. Whatever the case may be, we all have our reasons for getting into this profession, and the story behind why we felt called to it. Remind yourself of that reason whenever you feel discouraged or like this may not be for you. There is a reason . . . a 'why' . . . you became a teacher. Maybe where you are specifically isn't a good fit, but the heart of what you are doing is where you belong.

Inspiration from Students

Every teacher has students in their 'WHY' in some way, shape, or form. Knowing that we are influencing learners and helping them to succeed is often why we keep going. So how can we know if we are truly impacting students unless we take the time to get to know them in authentic ways? When we truly know our students and can help them with more than just their schoolwork, then we can see the impact we are having and be inspired to keep going on to the next day, week, and year.

Connecting with Students

You may think that you are "connected" with your students. But you will be surprised how much they haven't shared with you. Ask them what they wish *you* knew. Let them know that they can trust you, that you are here for them. You will be surprised how children of all ages react when you ask them, "What is something you wish I knew about you."

I Wish My Teacher Knew by Kyle Schwartz

This activity is a great way to reach out to your kiddos and remind yourself why you teach. Administering the "I wish my teacher knew. . ." activity is quite simple, really. Both Hannah S. and Dr. Sam carried the task out with their learners as a way to show compassion and empathy towards learners and to connect with students. Here is a rundown of the activity. Are you ready?

Materials: Writing utensil and paper: Sticky notes, notecards, or paint strip sample paper

Instructions:

- Simply give your learners a template or statement of "I wish my teacher knew. . ."
- Have the students complete the statement. It is completely open-ended.

That's it! Little to no prep! Of course, prepping your learners beforehand is a good idea, especially for the younger students. Explain to your students that completing this activity is a way for the teacher to learn more about each individual. Students may share whatever they wish to share with their teacher. Sometimes it may be something surface level, other times, it gets deep. Remind them that their responses will be kept private. Friends, please honor this. Keep the responses private UNLESS it is a situation where the student is planning to harm themselves or others. Students may or may not want to put their name on the paper. Students may want to share or keep their responses between them and the teacher. Some responses we received included: 'I think you are a great teacher,' 'I got a dog last week,' 'My grandma passed away last month, and I am still sad,' and 'I passed my spelling test.' As you can see, responses vary, but these can provide you with a lens into the lives of your students, and you can follow up. These prompts will also help you rethink your WHY.

Everything is better with an example, right? So, here we go. Let's say that little Johnny is having a bad day, a bad two days, a bad week. You try talking to him, but he won't open up and says that everything is fine. At the conclusion of the class, the students complete "I wish my teacher knew. . ." and while reading responses, you put two-and-two together and realize that Johnny's family is going through some tough stuff. That is the reason for him being "off" all week.

Checking in Regularly

Or, it's a Friday, and you pass out the weekly reflection as Hannah S. has done in the past. Weekly reflections are powerful tools! Part of the reflection this particular day was an "I wish my teacher knew. . ." portion. After reading several responses, Hannah learned that several of her students were excited about the football game and cheerleading at the game. Some were excited about the weekend for other fun events. Once Hannah read the responses, she was able to talk with her learners on Monday morning about why they were excited or not excited about the weekend. She was able to connect to her students on a personal level, and having that connection is important! Being real and open with students, and being someone that they can go to and feel safe with is one of the biggest things you can do for your students.

An additional way to connect with your learners is through a daily check-in using a form tool (Google or Microsoft forms should do the trick). This check-in helps students focus and reflect. You can customize it for your own class and students too. It helps to inform the teacher what is going on in the lives of students. Mari Venturino even provides you with a template that you can use and personalize it! So, check it out (Venturino, 2017).

Weekly Check In

Dr. Sam uses a similar method to gauge students at the end of each week. She lets her students know that the survey is voluntary but not anonymous. Dr. Sam states, "It is important to have student information attached to responses so she can reach out individually or one-on-one to a student." She lets students know that they complete it anytime and anywhere, and again, it is voluntary. If they choose to complete it, students fill in both short answer and Likert Scale-type responses. The short answer responses: how are you today, and how are things outside of class? This gives her a pulse on the students to track how they are each Friday, and what outside influences are coming at them that week or in the coming weeks. This helps to see if students are feeling stressed or overwhelmed in her class or other classes. . . or if things are just peachy! The next four questions are Likert Scale questions where students rate (through stars) her performance in each area related to getting to know them as individuals, clarity on topics, tools, and strategies, and if the weeks' topics helped students think more deeply about the content through discussion and assignments. The last question is a catch-all type question where she simply asks if there is anything that she needs to know.

Friends, this method above described by Dr. Sam is great for high school and adult learners, but you can also do check-ins with younger students and students with special needs by implementing an emotions pictograph (Reneau, 2019). Essentially, there are several feelings listed on the board, students write their name on the back of a sticky note (so their name is hidden), and they put their name where they are feeling that day. Students can do this while doing the mundane (or marvelous) morning routines.

Virtual Check In

By completing these activities daily, weekly, or monthly, you will not only feel more connected, but you WILL be more connected in a special way to your learners. By doing so, hopefully, you will realize that teaching is far more than the delivery of standards and content. By connecting with your learners, learning about their mental health, you will have a better understanding of how to adequately meet their emotional needs, ultimately helping your sanity as well.

Inspiration from Others

Ok, so you know your WHY, but you are just having a moment, a day, that you wonder where your WHY went. You are *deep* in the desert of teaching with no fountain in sight. . . how are you supposed to be refreshed? You don't feel that fulfilled, fruitful, this-is-why-I-teach feeling. Can we be honest? That's not uncommon. Like life, teaching will not always be a walk in the park. Before we give you some strategies for those unfilling days, think about a time when you were having a rough moment. How do you keep your head up? How do you keep yourself going? How do you find fulfillment in things when you are wondering what your purpose is?

What you jotted down will probably come in handy for those tough moments at school when the feeling of inspiration seems distant. Maybe you journal, go for a walk and think, work out, veg out and watch Netflix, get a fancy drink at the local coffee shop, speak to a therapist, go to a place of worship, etc. Whatever it is, you need to take care of you, especially on those rough days when you wonder why you became a teacher. Hopefully, those days are few and far between. But, at some point in your career, you will need to find inspiration when inspiration is lost. Here are some ways that we have found others who can speak into your life and your teaching and help you find that cool, refreshing inspiration.

Go-To Sources and Reminders

Who do you go to when you need inspiration? Who inspires you? What are some motivational quotes you constantly turn to? What are inspirational words that move you?

People Who Inspire Me	Quotes & Words That Inspire Me

Have these people and words handy. Talk things through. Walk it off and meditate on inspiration. Keep quotes on your desk or walls. Aspire to inspire yourself.

Bringing Back Your PLN

Don't stop at the familiar people to look for inspiration. Step outside your comfort zone and connect with other educators. There are two ways in which you can accomplish this, and the first is through social media. If you have taken Dr. Sam's EDUC 204 Technology of Instruction course or read *EduMagic: A Guide for Preservice Teachers* (Fecich, 2018), then you will already understand the importance of social media for educators. Building a professional presence online is a great opportunity to collaborate and share educational ideas and practices. It is also a great source of classroom, professional development, and self-motivating inspiration. Just remember, you are your own person and your own educator. As you find inspiration from others, don't compare yourself to them but learn from others to help you grow.

Get Connected: Three reasons why you need to get connected today!

Educators across the 'gram, Facebook, and Twitter provide a wide range of ideas, tips, and tricks (oh my!). Sometimes it is just refreshing and inspirational to take a moment to admire the #edumagic and #megapixel moments other educators foster in their settings. There are several profiles and hashtags out there that are simply motivational outlooks for teachers. These are some of our favs, but be sure to find some that you love to add to the list!

- #Newteacher
- #NT2T
- #NTchat
- #Teacherinspiration
- #EduMagic
- #Kidsdeserveit
- #NewTeachers

Top Five Ways to Connect Online (in any order)

Podcasts

- Listen to short audio segments while getting ready in the morning. Want some podcast recommendations? Check out Dr. Sam's blog post QR in Chapter 1!

Twitter Chats

- Grow professionally during those long commercials of your favorite TV episodes. . . invest in yourself!

How do I rock my first Twitter chat?

Online Book Studies

- I mean, we all read poolside in the summer, right?! Or by the beach with a fun drink? Book studies occur year-round and are based on a variety of books for educators. Check out #bookcamppd for more information and jump into your favorite teacher read with peers!

Facebook Groups

- Share ideas and resources, and get your questions answered.

Blogs

- Downloads, downloads, downloads! PLUS some great stories and ideas, tips, and tricks.

Going Offline and Into the Real World

Another way to connect with other educators for inspiration beyond profiles and hashtags is to connect with in-person professional development. Did you ever go to a camp or event and feel that fire within you? That is an amazing feeling! Get involved with conferences and learning opportunities that allow you to be involved with others like you. Feed off each other for inspiration. Listen to their stories, their experiences, their lessons. We promise, you know it was a good conference when you leave feeling refreshed, ignited for learning, passionate about teaching, and inspired.

So how can you get started with in-person PD? First, think about professional development style. . . do you like to attend conferences, or do you enjoy having a conversation one on one with another educator? There is no right answer here- we have resources for everyone! You can attend conferences in your niche. Just Google the national or international organization that fits your needs, and they most likely have a conference or gathering each year. An opposite vibe of traditional presentations is an Edcamp. Edcamps are referred to as unconferences, meaning that sessions aren't planned until the day of the event. During an edcamp participants are given a sticky note, and on that note, you write down which areas of education you want to learn more about . . . let's try it out.

Once you write down the topic, you stick it on a board or give it to a volunteer. Volunteers then take everyone's notes and organize the day based on topics. Instead of lectures and presentations, attendees engage in conversation around the topic areas to learn more. The day is full of high energy and excitement. It is a lot of fun to attend an Edcamp. . . the four of us were so inspired by the first one we attended together that it led to us founding one!

Maybe you are more of a small group type person; if that's the case, then CoffeeEDUs are your jam! CoffeeEDUs are at a local gathering place where teachers chat about the areas of education that they are most passionate about. To find out more about CoffeeEDU, check out their website or search #CoffeeEDU! Who doesn't love a cup of coffee and chat with educators?

CoffeeEDU	Edcamp

Finding Fellow Learners

Another way to feel the inspiration to teach and re-engage with your WHY is to become involved in continuing education. This may be as simple as taking one class, or it could be enrolling in a degree program. Either way, when you surround yourself with others who want to learn how to be the best educators they can be, you will feel the passion for teaching.

Ah, going back to school—who wants to hear that after receiving a diploma? Going back to school can take two paths: some teachers go right back to school into a master's program, and some pursue their master's degree while also diving headfirst into the classroom. Dr. Sam is one of those first ones. After receiving her Bachelor of Education in December, she went back to school in the following fall to receive a master's degree in special education, specializing in augmentative and alternative communication. She worked very hard and completed her masters in a residential campus in one year. She was also awarded a graduate assistantship to help defray costs. This was an incredible learning experience where she could immerse herself into a passion area and dig deep into learning and growing.

Hannah S. followed the second path in pursuing post-undergrad education. As previously mentioned, she decided to start her Master of Education program during the fall of her second year of teaching. Hannah reflects back to a book used for a course, a book entitled *Why We Teach Now* by Sonia Nieto (2014). This book was full of personal stories from educators about their WHYs. "It was emotional, engaging, and inspiring to read," Hannah states. She goes on to say that collaborating with colleagues during her twelve-month journey as a graduate student was inspirational. She explains,

 You are in a class with other educators who are just like you, continuing their education for some reason or another. Sometimes the eagerness to learn is very evident; other times, not so much. Regardless, sharing stories and experiences with other educators who may have been teaching for longer than I have been alive is so unique! Those teachers have taught, literally, my whole life and have witnessed diverse changes in education from curriculum to student life. Being able to learn from and with those educators made me excited for learning. I wanted to learn the best practices for my students. I wanted to foster the passion and immersion into teaching that I saw in my colleagues. In a way, going back to school inspired me to become a better educator."

Feeling Refreshed?

Friends, in this chapter, we shared several ways to keep the fire going when it comes to owning your professional development and learning. We would like you to take some time to reflect on some areas you are passionate about in education. How can you learn more and pursue your passions? Maybe it's going back to school or attending a webinar. Write it down below and brainstorm how you can accomplish that goal!

Now, create some goals: goals that are Specific, Measurable, Attainable, Relevant, and Timely are the SMART way to write goals (Hitt, S., 2017). Maybe you came across some really cool techniques or resources that you want to incorporate into your classroom . . . this is the place to make goals to help you accomplish that!

Rewrite your WHY:

Come back later and reflect on these goals and your WHY. Has your WHY changed? Did you go back to school? Did you attend a webinar? Did you connect? Be reflective throughout this EduMagic journey and watch the sprinkles scatter!

8

C: Check Yo'self

As our journey together ends, we want to leave you with a few more tips, specifically on how to be the best possible version of yourself. Living and learning the teaching experience is very rewarding, but will also sometimes come with unfilled expectations, disappointments, and a long to-do list. Friends, those are all part of life. Some circumstances may make it easy to complain or take things personally. Others may make you feel small and incompetent. Pessimism and low self-esteem will only hinder you from being present and 'in-tune' with your students. You must find a way to check your attitude and build yourself back up.

Build Up #1: Get Up Again. . . and Again. . .

Remember those Teacher Expectations in Chapter 1? Most first-year teachers have a similar outlook on how the year will start and how they will work with coworkers in a wonderful way. Maybe you can relate to this. . . picture it in slow motion: walking down the halls, waving to every teacher—confidently dressed to impress, everyone smiling and enjoying the week before students return and getting to work. Every teacher- ready to share their ideas and to brainstorm new thoughts to teach students new concepts. This would be the picture-perfect situation for collaborating with coworkers productively to strive to help each learner in the school building. However, it rarely looks quite this picturesque.

The first year of teaching is beneficial and has taught each of us so much. It has helped us grow as educators in so many ways. It stretched us and molded us into the educators we are today. As you have read, we all have worked through many challenges in our classroom, and we also had great days that brought tears of joy to our eyes and smiles to our faces. Not every day is going to be sunshine and flowers; you will have days that are just okay, and days that just stink for one reason or another. And that is OK. Seriously, it is OK that you have those days. Allow yourself to be OK with that now. Through it all, you are unstoppable. You will pick up your feet and try again tomorrow.

Shayla S. spent her first three years teaching in Ghana, and faced several challenges in getting started, some that were seemingly impossible to overcome! She shares her realization that sometimes we have to work within difficult circumstances, and the most important thing is to give our personal best within those circumstances.

 I realized that the bar I set for myself was actually too high and unrealistic, given my situation. I had one week to unpack my things, begin adapting to a new country, learn all the procedures and policies of the school, and begin setting up my classroom with limited resources. My job changed from first-grade teacher to Special Education K-12 teacher three days before school began. How was I going to submit my lesson plans for the first week of school when I was still figuring out what my new position entailed? How would I create a lesson before I knew my students and what their needs were? I soon discovered that flexibility, adaptability, and quickness to learn were going to be much more important to me than writing full lesson plans and meeting deadlines. I learned that many schools are less 'put-together' than they first look and that I needed to be content with giving my personal best within that.

Whether it's reality or not, I left college feeling like I was expecting to be perfect as a first-year teacher. I had to quickly accept that I wasn't going to be near perfect, or maybe even acceptable in my college's eyes, but that it is okay. It's okay to plan day-by-day for the first semester. It's okay to not get the lesson plans turned in at first. It's okay to admit to your principal and fellow teachers that you don't know what to do, and you need help. I learned that people give me grace much more easily than I give myself grace. People want to help. Although I felt that my college demanded perfection, my school did not."

Shayla went on to teach in Ghana for two more years, creating a special education curriculum to use, and teaching and loving many students. So, friends, when you are struck down and discouraged by whatever situation or circumstance you may be in, remember that you are not alone, and you WILL be able to keep going!

Make Magic Happen:

On the days when your expectations have not been fulfilled, have a mantra or reminder to yourself that tomorrow is a new day to grow and learn from, and that today was just a learning experience. What is something you can say to remind yourself that tomorrow is a new day, a new lesson, and a new unit? Write down your personal reminder to 'just keep swimming' (Stanton, Unkrich, Brooks, DeGeneres, & Gould, 2013)!

Build Up #2: Be Positively Yourself!

Unfortunately, you will run into negative people. . . you know, those Debby Downers. Sometimes they might be upset with their students, angry with another individual or an event that has nothing to do with school. Occasionally they may bring their issues into their classrooms or take it out on their coworkers and in their team discussions. We are not saying it is not okay to ever have a bad day at work, what we are saying it is unhealthy to be negative for long periods.

So, how do you stay positive when things get negative? Katy shares about an encounter the week before school started that tested this positive consistency. According to Katy, it felt like an episode in the Netflix T.V. show *Nailed It!* (Starkman, 2018). You may remember that episode where Nicole Byer takes a bite of a cupcake expecting a sweet surprise; however, she was shocked when she found that the chef used salt instead of sugar. Nicole calls for Wes, her assistant, to get her some water and leaves the non-expert chef saying sarcastically, "This has been a journey."

Katy is sure Ms. Byer was left with a bad taste in her mouth, just as Katy was with her first negative comment. The comment was said during a discussion with two other educators about how Katy was prepared to start the year. The teachers both gave Katy a weird look and said, "Try not to be too happy, you don't want to smile until after Christmas." Have you ever heard this phrase spoken in the halls of your classroom? Katy G. says, "I really was in disbelief. Apparently, this is a common saying; however, until this point, I had never heard of it." This technique might work for some individuals, but that's not Katy's style or what she was taught as best practice. Katy says, "I started to question EVERYTHING, and school was about to begin in two weeks! I was thinking, 'OMG, these middle school kids are going to eat me alive. I am too bubbly!'"

Friends, the most important thing you can be is *yourself*. If you are so busy trying to perform for your students and colleagues, you will be way too tired to actually teach. If you are a happy, bubbly person, BE that person! Being firm and having structure is important, but that doesn't mean you need to be stern all the time. In fact, saving the 'stern' voice and face for the moments that need it will give it more impact in those moments, rather than the whole school year just being a montage of how mean you are all the time. Hannah T. likens it to parenting; teaching your kid and correcting your kid are two very different tones, and if you are going to effectively do either of those things you need to be able to know when to use the 'it's okay to make mistakes' voice and the 'mom' voice. You will find your different voices throughout the school year, but the important thing is to make them *your* voices.

Build Up #3: Learn from Mistakes

In your first year, you are going to look back and wish you had reacted differently in some situations. This is so common and is honestly how we grow as educators. There was one circumstance that stuck with Katy G. from her first year:

> I have played this case over and over in my head on how I could have done better for my student: While teaching, a student needed to use the restroom. I am not a stickler about not letting students using the bathroom; however, my students do know I give them a set time to return. On one particular day, my student, we will call him Robert, had to use the restroom. He was a frequent bathroom user, but he always returned at the appropriate time. Coincidentally, the student was at my door with one of my colleagues. We can call this teacher Mr. Feely. Mr. Feely decided to take the opportunity to let me know how Robert was behaving in the hallway. I stood there and listened to his point of view because I was trying to be supportive.

Unfortunately, it became a very negative experience and was degrading to my student. Mr. Feely told me that Robert told him that he was not his teacher and did not have to listen to him. Mr. Feely continued yelling at Robert at my classroom door for everyone to hear. It disrupted the learning environment, and it was belittling to Robert. Robert entered the classroom after we both thought the discussion was over. Mr. Feely came into my room to yell at him again and to tell him that he would never pass the 7th grade and would be held back. I was frozen because I was in disbelief that this event just occurred in my classroom. The teacher left, and Robert was left defeated even though he put on a tough front.

I finished class, and then I pulled him aside. Robert was one of my goofy students, but never disrespectful. So, I was confused about his confrontation with Mr. Feely. He informed me that Mr. Feely told him and his friend to get back to class. Robert acknowledged the teacher and bid farewell to his friend. It must have not been quick enough for Mr. Feely, so he made a comment that Robert did not take kindly. Robert quickly responded to the teacher that he does not have to listen to him because Mr. Feely was not his teacher. I explained to Robert that even though he might not have agreed with Mr. Feely, there is still no reason to talk to an adult in this manner.

I explained to Robert that when he has a job one day, he will not always get along with his coworkers, but he still needs to be respectful. When I work with middle school students, using job references really helps them put situations into perspective. I continued to talk with Robert about the comment that Mr. Feely made toward him about being held back. I told him there might be teachers that he will come across in the future that will discourage him, make him want to give up, or talk down to him. There is a difference in being tough toward students to help them better themselves, and being completely disrespectful. I told Robert that Mr. Feely was in the wrong, and Robert should not believe what he told him. I told him that I believed in him, and he should show this teacher that he was wrong to ever insinuate that he would not pass the seventh grade based on appearance and a one-time interaction.

Even with my efforts, the student still returned the next day to talk about the incident. He went home to talk to his family about it too. The student was in such disarray about the comments the teacher made toward him the day before. I tried to reassure my student, but I knew it would take time for this individual to heal."

This was such an impactful event during Katy's first year because she wished so dearly that she could have changed the events that occurred that day for this student. She wished she could go back and tell the teacher that was an inappropriate comment to make towards her student. She can't go back and change this event; however, she can learn from it. Understanding how it impacted her student, and how the words we say as teachers can stick throughout the rest of our students' lives, makes it all the more important that we choose our words carefully and never say things we later regret. We are sure that you remember some impactful words, both good and bad, from educators in your life.

Katy G. continued to stay positive because she was happy, she was able to provide a safe space for this student to come speak to her. It is not every day that a 13-year-old wants to talk to an adult and ask questions. She loved it! She was happy that she could learn from this experience to ensure that, to the best of her ability, she would never let it happen again. Sometimes as a first-year teacher, it is more beneficial to look at the bright side and celebrate what you are doing correctly.

David S. shares an inspiring story to remind us just how much students take our words to heart:

> The last day of school was also a wonderful encouragement as an educator. Students recalled things I had said and how I encouraged them at the beginning of the school year, phrases and words I had almost forgotten. I was reminded that the students notice some of the smallest details and that they remember. They take to heart words of hurt and encouragement. At the very end of the last day, I asked students to sign my yearbook. One young lady who was kind and caring while struggling with self-image and self-confidence wrote the following sentence in my yearbook. 'Thank you for teaching me not only science, but also how to live.' This is my hope for every student who walks through my classroom door."

Friends, let the words that your students remember be words that will build them up through their school career and even their whole life! Little (and big) ears are listening and processing everything we say, from reading to relationships. It may feel like a lot of pressure to be perfect, but we can always have grace with ourselves and correct mistakes when we need to. If we are staying positive and being in a positive place, our actions and words will reflect that for our students!

Build Up #4: Kids Will Be Kids

If you haven't realized yet, kids are simply that: kids. They are still learning and growing in maturity, and often can't understand, process, and reason through situations the way we can as adults. It's unreasonable to expect a six- or seven-year-old to always make the right choice in situations, and similarly for a 13- to 16-year-old. Hannah T. once had to ask a first grader why he colored his teeth with a crayon. . . his answer? "I don't know." He really didn't have any idea why he had done it! That is how kids are: impulsive. It's part of what makes them kids!

They also cannot help their situation and the life that was handed to them. Maybe their families can't help it either. Life can be hard and perplexing. Students of all ages are faced with hardships that are out of their control: drugs, poverty, challenges at home, etc. Once you immerse yourself into the demographics, one can easily see how difficult life can be for the children in our lives. Before you get frustrated that little Tommy did not study for the test or Suzy never returned the permission form, consider the situation that these kiddos may be in. Maybe Tommy has to get up, pack his lunch, do the chores, and make breakfast all in time to make the bus. Or, maybe Suzy is going between three homes.

Now, we'll be the first to admit that some days, this is just so hard to do! It can be so easy to start grumbling because Johnny is never prepared, or Pete is cursing again. You may find yourself reprimanding a child for swearing, only to learn that swearing is normal at home. You may have to remind a student, yet again, to "Stop and think!" before doing something. But every day they mature a little more, and the goal is the struggles that a six-year-old has are not the same struggles the 16-year-old faces.

Needless to say, before you get frustrated about behaviors or irresponsibility, remember that not every child is in a home where academics are a priority, and every child is a work in progress to become a mature adult.

Build Up #5: Cheer Yourself On

Sometimes you may feel alone because you are the new kid on the block. You are probably walking into a department or wing where the other teachers already have their friendship and "with-it-ness" about them. Most likely, and hopefully, you are cheerfully welcomed in by your new colleagues. But, once that honeymoon phase is over and the weeks pass by, the feeling of being alone surfaces.

One friend shares,

 There were certainly times that I felt alone. I looked around at other teachers who had their best friends and who seemed to have it all together. I mean, they ate lunch in the teacher's lounge! And left by 4:30! And looking at their Twitter feeds, they were doing amazing things in their classroom. . . something I was continually reminded of in team meetings and from others who were always praising them. I just wanted one small win, just one. Just one person to notice that I was trying my hardest to help my students succeed while flying by the seat of my pants.

The one time that I specifically remember someone encouraging me in a really specific way (because a generic 'you're doing great!' only goes so far) was when a team member across the hall came into my room and, in a very real way, told me that I really had grown a lot and I had 'found my confidence'. It really meant a lot to me that she noticed, and that she saw it as a plus that I was feeling confident and starting to try new things. I had others who would encourage me along the way as well, always when I was really discouraged and not feeling very supported or encouraged. But ultimately, I learned to be my own biggest cheerleader and find my own successes to celebrate. If no one knew my students as well as me, then no one could possibly celebrate their achievements as well as me. So even when the results weren't on paper, I knew that there was growth happening in my classroom and that I wasn't the big failure it sometimes seemed."

You may *feel* like you are a loner, but people are watching from the sidelines. Unfortunately, you may not always hear them cheering. It's kind of like a sports game. . . bear with us a moment. Envision that you are a coach on the bench with the athletes and the fans wildly cheering. However, no one on the field can actually *hear* what is being cheered. It's halftime, your team is losing, and your athletes are looking at you for some encouragement. You think for a moment and realize that your team is actually doing great! So many great gains have been made on defense throughout the season, and the offense has become very aggressive! Your colleagues are the fans, your students are athletes, and you are the coach. You may not be able to hear your peers, but you know your students' gains and your own growth. Celebrate what others don't know and grow!

Make Magic Happen:

Take time at specific points in the year to mark growth and goals. Maybe at the beginning or end of every month, or every marking period. Think about any personal or life goals you have for you or any of your students, and some academic goals you have for them. Write down the goals and then check on them as the year goes on to see how students really *have* grown in measurable ways. Even when you may fall short of your goals, still be sure to mark where there has been positive growth. Yes, Johnny didn't grow 3 reading levels to get where he needed to be, but he did grow 1, almost 2! He knows all his blends now and doesn't get tripped up on sight words! Take intentional time throughout the school year to celebrate and write down the positives to keep yourself encouraged with upward growth!

Checking Your Attitude Reminders

- Don't take things personally.

- Don't forget your WHY! Go back and remind yourself why you are doing this.
- Seek to understand: Be slow to speak, quick to listen, quicker to think. Always try to be an active listener, so you can add a positive spin. Listen actively, engage in conversation, and try not to space out.
- What would you do? Do you agree with what was said? Why or why not? What will you do because of that?
- Surround yourself with positive people and/or people you aspire to be like (Twitter, friends from school, former professors-turned-friends, etc.). Meaning, find positive co-workers, follow positive educators on social media, read empowering books, etc. You know that saying your mom told you about, "birds of a feather flock together"? It is so true.
- Get inspired! Go back and review who and what inspires you. Look at your past experiences and remind yourself of the times you were inspired. Create an inspiration board on Pinterest with positive phrases and encouraging words.
- Take a look at your classroom and think of the positive sayings any of your students have said to you, or be like Dr. Sam and keep a drawer of positive notes, cards, and sticky notes! If you don't have a drawer start one.
- Find that person or people you can be real with.
- Be mindful of your reactions. Everyone has bad days. . . and that's okay. You are going to have a bad lesson, day, or week, and it is OK to acknowledge that. But it is how you react that makes the difference. Don't be that teacher with a rain cloud over their head. . . how will you bounce back from a setback?
- Be mindful of the journey that your students are experiencing. Be there for them and seek to understand.
- Friends, you are unstoppable! Don't forget that! Stay true to yourself, stay humble, and never stop growing.

Make Your Magic Happen!

We hope that this book provided you with valuable insight, reflective thoughts, and lots of tips to help you through this journey of being a new teacher. We urge you to use this guidebook as just that: a guide. Use every square centimeter of white space and get reflective! While we definitely hope that this workbook is helpful to you and you use it to reflect throughout the year, we also recommend having another journal, blog, or something with more space to reflect on your experience. Maybe use Instagram to post your thoughts at the end of each day or tweet out a daily thought on Twitter. Whatever it is, don't wait for a special day or event to remember the day. Every day in itself is special and deserves to be documented in some small way. You can write out paragraphs or bullet points or even a drawing of your day. Try to document something from each day. . . you won't regret it!

Hannah T. shares that she had a journal she really loved, and ironically ended up not writing in very much because she wanted to save it for 'profound' thoughts and reflections. But friends. . . your reflections are profound! Your experiences, failures, and successes are all part of growing you and making you a better teacher, and it is important to remember and reflect on all of them. Hannah T. regrets not writing in her notebook regularly, even if it was just one win/growth a day.

One more thing that you need is a drawer or box where you keep all of your mementos from your students. From being a first-year teacher all the way through to being a professor, Dr. Sam has kept a drawer full of notes and letters from students in years past. She reads them over when she is feeling down or having a bad day, and they immediately help her refocus on her why and put the students first. She encourages you to do the same. Keep those notes, drawings, letters, and slips of paper that are given to you by students. Put the small tokens of their love and appreciation around your classroom. When you look at the item, it will give you a quick thought of that student and put a smile on your face. Dr. Sam keeps items around her office from students throughout the years. Looking at each item helps her to remember that student, focus on her why, and, of course, smile!

Your first year of teaching is unlike any other. It is the first and last time you will have your first classroom. The first year will test you as a teacher, and it will also bring you tremendous joy. You are shaping the lives of students, and you've got this! You can do this! This is a tough job, and it is a big job, but you can do it. You are strong. You are bright. You are a teacher! Be amazing, and believe in yourself.

Remember sharing is caring- show how you are letting your inner *Edumagic* shine by posting on Instagram or Twitter with #EdumagicNT.

9

Special Thanks

A VERY SPECIAL thanks to these #Eduawesome Edumagicians who contributed their thoughts and stories.

Maddie Bowser

Maddie B. is an elementary teacher who describes her first year with the word *grow*. She cautions you to not compare yourself to other teachers. "We are all unique, and it's okay to achieve the same goal differently."

Abby McLain

Abby M. is a special education teacher. Echoing the importance of finding mentors, Abby truthfully states that she would have likely quit teaching if she hadn't found quality work friends who encouraged, pushed, and listened to her. Thankfully, Abby found her people and those who help her through the journey.

. . .

Shayla Schafhauser

Shayla S. spent three years in Ghana, Africa. That experience alone brought challenges. During her time, Shayla was both an elementary teacher and a special education teacher. Shayla kindly reminds new teachers that it is ok to be in a messy position or in a school that is struggling. "No school is perfect, and no teacher is perfect."

David Shang

David S. is a middle school teacher who reminds us that drastic changes rarely "occur by one person at one moment, but through the consistency of many people in many daily tasks." Growth and change are desired, but will take time with healthy amounts of confidence and humility.

Abby Trypus

Abby T. is the coordinator at an Intermediate Unit who shares that her first year was a journey, starting her career with a husband and one-year-old at home. She realized that organization and balance between work and home was important. "Your job is important, and it's important to do it to the best of your ability, but your family time is more important."

New teachers, this one's for you! This book is dedicated to all of the new teachers around the world who are starting their journey into the best career on the planet!

Shoutouts

From Hannah T:

For the professors and friends who gave me the tools to teach, the students and colleagues who taught me how to use them, and the family who supported me while I learned more than I ever had before.

From Hannah S:

To Dr. Linda Culbertson and Dr. Sam Fecich, who ignited my passion for learning and teaching. To my students who humble me and help me grow as an educator. To Karen, Cassey, and Loretta, who have answered my many "Question!"s and have become my work family. Most importantly, to my family, who are my constant cheerleaders. Mom and Dad, I wouldn't be where I am today without your loving guidance, support, and the wings that you have given me.

From Katy G:

For my PawPaw and MawMaw, thank you for teaching me to be kind to others, have a strong work ethic, to be a listener, and to never give up. You both were my biggest cheerleaders, and I appreciate you both more than you will ever know.

From Sam F: To Josh Fecich and Summer Lee Fecich- you are the loves of my life. Thank you for your constant love, support, and encouragement.

Dr. Sam Fecich: I'm a professor of education at a liberal arts college in western Pennsylvania, USA. I work with future teachers each day in the areas of educational technology and special education. I also have the honor of supervising some of our student teachers. I am the author of *EduMagic: A Guide for Preservice Teachers* and the host of the podcast: EduMagic—a podcast designed with future teachers in mind.

Katy Gibson: I am currently a sixth-grade science and social studies teacher in Pennsylvania. I have taught seventh-grade math and science, been a paraprofessional (fifth-sixth) in a learning support classroom, and a fifth-grade long-term substitute. I graduated from Grove City College in 2017 with a B.S. in Middle Level (fourth-eighth) Math and Science degree.

Hannah Sansom: I graduated from Grove City College in 2016 and was blessed with getting hired that summer. This year marks year four as the third-grade math teacher. I am dually certified in elementary and special education and have my Master of Education degree in Reading and Math.

Hannah Turk: I graduated from Grove City College in 2016 with a B.S. Elementary (PK-4) and Special (PK-8) Education degree. I taught first grade at a Title I school in Northern Virginia for my first year of teaching. Since the birth of my daughter on the last day of school (so close!), I have been at home teaching with a 1-1 student teacher ratio, although as of November 2019, the ratio has changed to 1-2. I am currently part of the moderating team for the Twitter chat #NT2t (New Teachers to Twitter). Whenever I get the chance, I like to read, stream movies and TV, and continue studying early child development up close and personal.

References

Couros, G. (2016, February). *Pete&C. PETE&C*. Hershey, PA.

Fecich, S. (2018). *Edumagic: a guide for pre-service teachers*. Alexandria, VA: EduMatch.

Danielson, C. (2007). *Enhancing professional practice: A framework for teaching*. Alexandria, VA: Association for Supervision and Curriculum Development.

Del Vecho, P. (Producer), & Lee, J. & Buck, C. (Directors). (2013). *Frozen* [Motion picture]. United States: Walt Disney Studios Motion Pictures.

GoNoodle. (2019). Retrieved September 2, 2019, from https://www.gonoodle.com/

Hitt, S. (2017, August 11). Setting S.M.A.R.T. Goals as an Educator. Retrieved from https://achievethecore.org/aligned/setting-s-m-a-r-t-goals-as-an-educator/

Kondo, M., & Hirano, C. (2014). *The life-changing magic of tidying up*. London: Vermilion.

Nieto, S. (2014). *Why we teach now*. New York, NY: Teachers College Press.

Reneau, A. (2019, April 1). *This teacher's viral 'check-in' board is a beautiful example of mental health support*. (2019). *Upworthy*. Retrieved 4 September 2019, from https://www.upworthy. com/this-teacher-s-viral-check-in-board-is-a-beautiful-example-of-mental-health-support

Sansom, H. (2016, November 23). |Inadequate|. [Blog post]. Retrieved 4 September 2019, from https:// multiplyinglearning4all.wordpress.com/2016/ 11/23/inadequate/

Sansom, H. (2017). Grove City Talk. Personal Collection of H. Sansom.

Schain, D. (Producer), & Ortega, K. (Directors). (2006). *High School Musical* [Motion picture]. United States: Walt Disney Studios Motion Pictures.

Spencer, C. (Producer), & Moore, R. (Director). (2012). *Wreck-it Ralph!* [Motion Picture]. United States: Walt Disney Studios.

Stanton, A., Unkrich, L., Brooks, A., DeGeneres, E., & Gould, A. (2013). *Finding Nemo*. [video recording]. Burbank, CA: Walt Disney Studios Home Entertainment, 2013.

Starkman, P. (Director). (2018, June 29). Fictitious and Delicious [Television Series Episode] In D. Cutforth & J. Lipsitz (Producers), *Nailed It!* Netflix.

Tolkien, J. R. (1954). *Fellowship of the Ring.* George Allen & Unwin.

Unions and Management Partnerships - Center for American Progress. (2014). Center for American Progress. Retrieved 2 September 2019, from https://www.americanprogress.org/issues/education-k-12/reports/2014/03/25/86332/teachers-unions-and-management-partnerships/

Venturino, M. (2017). *Daily Check-in with Google Forms. Mari Venturino.* Retrieved 4 September 2019, from https://mariventurino.com/2017/10/13/daily-check-in-with-google-forms/

Woolfolk, A. (2013). *Educational Psychology.* (12th ed., p. 59). New Jersey: Pearson

EduMagic by Sam Fecich

This book challenges the thought that "teaching" begins only after certification and college graduation. Instead, it describes how students in teacher preparation programs have value to offer their future colleagues, even as they are learning to be teachers!

EduMatch Snapshot in Education (2016)
In this collaborative project, twenty educators located throughout the United
States share educational strategies that have worked well for them, both with
students and in their professional practice.

The #EduMatch Teacher's Recipe Guide
Editors: Tammy Neil & Sarah Thomas
Dive in as fourteen international educators share their recipes for success,
both literally and metaphorically!

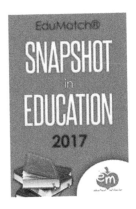

EduMatch Snapshot in Education (2017)
We're back! EduMatch proudly presents Snapshot in Education (2017). In this two-volume collection, 32 educators and one student share their tips for the classroom and professional practice.

Journey to The "Y" in You by Dene Gainey
This book started as a series of separate writing pieces that were eventually woven together to form a fabric called The Y in You. The question is, "What's the 'why' in you?"

The Teacher's Journey by Brian Costello
Follow the Teacher's Journey with Brian as he weaves together the stories of seven incredible educators. Each step encourages educators at any level to reflect, grow, and connect.

The Fire Within
Compiled and edited by Mandy Froehlich
Adversity itself is not what defines us. It is how we react to that adversity and the choices we make that creates who we are and how we will persevere.

Makers in Schools
Editors: Susan Brown & Barbara Liedahl
The maker mindset sets the stage for the Fourth Industrial Revolution,
empowering educators to guide their students.

Divergent EDU by Mandy Froehlich
The concept of being innovative can be made to sound so simple. But what if
the development of the innovative thinking isn't the only roadblock?

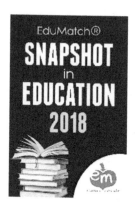

EduMatch Snapshot in Education (2018)
EduMatch® is back for our third annual Snapshot in Education. Dive in as
21 educators share a snapshot of what they learned, what they did, and how
they grew in 2018.

Daddy's Favorites by Elissa Joy
Illustrated by Dionne Victoria
Five-year-old Jill wants to be the center of everyone's world. But, her most
favorite person in the world, without fail, is her Daddy. But Daddy has to be
Daddy, and most times that means he has to be there when everyone needs
him, especially when her brother Danny needs him.

Level Up Leadership by Brian Kulak
Gaming has captivated its players for generations and cemented itself as a fundamental part of our culture. In order to reach the end of the game, they all need to level up.

DigCit Kids edited by Marialice Curran & Curran Dee
This book is a compilation of stories, starting with our own mother and son story, and shares examples from both parents and educators on how they embed digital citizenship at home and in the classroom. (Also available in Spanish)

Stories of EduInfluence by Brent Coley
In Stories of EduInfluence, veteran educator Brent Coley shares stories from more than two decades in the classroom and front office.

The Edupreneur by Dr. Will
The Edupreneur is a 2019 documentary film that takes you on a journey into the successes and challenges of some of the most recognized names in K-12 education consulting.

In Other Words by Rachelle Dene Poth
In Other Words is a book full of inspirational and thought-provoking quotes that have pushed the author's thinking and inspired her.

To Whom it May Concern
Editors: Sarah-Jane Thomas, PhD & Nicol R. Howard, PhD
In To Whom it May Concern..., you will read a collaboration between two Master's in Education classes at two universities on opposite coasts of the United States.

One Drop of Kindness by Jeff Kubiak
This children's book, along with each of you, will change our world as we
know it. It only takes One Drop of Kindness to fill a heart with love.

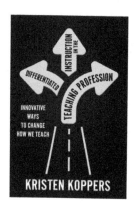

DI in the Teaching Profession by Kristen Koppers
Differentiated Instruction in the Teaching Profession is an innovative way to
use critical thinking skills to create strategies to help all students succeed.

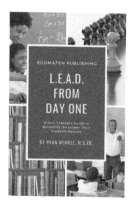

L.E.A.D. from Day One by Ryan McHale
L.E.A.D. from Day One is a go-to resource to help educators outline a future plan toward becoming a teacher leader.

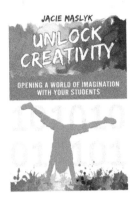

Unlock Creativity by Jacie Maslyk
Every classroom is filled with creative potential. Unlock Creativity will help you discover opportunities that will make every student see themselves as a creative thinker.

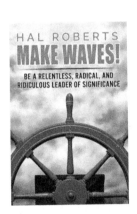

Make Waves! by Hal Roberts
In Make Waves! Hal discusses 15 attributes of a great leader. He shares his varied experience as a teacher, leader, a player in the N.F.L., and a plethora of research to take you on a journey to emerge as leader of significance.

21 Lessons of Tech Integration Coaching by Martine Brown
In 21 Lessons of Tech Integration Coaching, Martine Brown provides a practical guide about how to use your skills to support and transform schools.

EduMatch Publishing

Made in the USA
Middletown, DE
19 May 2020

95376583R00096